What
Stories
Does
My Son
Need?

PREVIOUS WORKS BY MICHAEL GURIAN

Parenting

The Good Son

A Fine Young Man

The Wonder of Boys

Psychology

Love's Journey

Mothers, Sons and Lovers

The Prince and the King

Young Adult Titles

Understanding Guys

From Boys to Men

Fiction

An American Mystic

PREVIOUS WORKS BY TERRY TRUEMAN

Stuck in Neutral

Sheehan

What Stories Does My Son Need?

A Guide to
Books and
Movies That
Build Character
in Boys

MICHAEL GURIAN WITH TERRY TRUEMAN

Jeremy P. Tarcher/Putnam
a member of Penguin Putnam Inc. New York

Most Tarcher/Putnam books are available at special quantity discounts for bulk purchase for sales promotions, premiums, fund-raising, and educational needs. Special books or book excerpts also can be created to fit specific needs. For details, write Putnam Special Markets, 375 Hudson Street, New York, NY 10014.

Jeremy P. Tarcher/Putnam
A member of
Penguin Putnam Inc.
375 Hudson Street
New York, NY 10014
www.penguinputnam.com

Library of Congress Cataloging-in-Publication Data

Gurian, Michael.
   What stories does my son need? : a guide to books
and movies that build character in boys / by Michael Gurian
with Terry Trueman.
     p.   cm.
   ISBN 1-58542-040-9
    1. Boys—Psychology.   2. Boys—Books and reading.
3. Motion pictures for children.   4. Mass media and
children.   5. Child rearing.   I. Trueman, Terry.   II. Title.
HQ775.G824   2000   00-023961
028.1'6241—dc21

Printed in the United States of America
10   9   8   7   6   5   4 ' 3   2   1

This book is printed on acid-free paper. ∞

Book design by Mauna Eichner

Acknowledgments

We would like to graciously thank Mitch Horowitz, Joel Fotinos, Ken Siman, and everyone at Tarcher/Putnam for their care with this project, as well as Susan Schulman for shepherding it through. Many thanks also to Stacie Wachholz for her help with essential portions of this project.

Our profound thanks go to all the authors and filmmakers who have focused humanity on moral and ethical issues. They inspire all of us to realize that though it is essential to entertain audiences, our *first* intention as creators of stories for children ought to be to teach ethics and worth to the next generation.

Dedicated to our children,

Gabrielle and Davita

and

Sheehan and Jesse

Contents

Elementary School

Lower Grades 1–3

Upper Grades 4–6

Middle School

High School   **59**

100 BOOKS

Preschool/Kindergarten

Elementary School   **91**

Lower Grades 1–3

Upper Grades 4–6

Middle School

High School   122

The Stories
a Boy Needs

One night my wife and I stood in line to see the brilliant but brutal war film *Saving Private Ryan.* In front of us stood a young man and woman and their four-year-old boy, and next to us, in the line for *Blade,* a gory horror-thriller, another young couple with their five-year-old son. Gail and I felt a familiar sadness, anger, and even fear: sadness because of the brutality the children would witness; protective anger at the children's caregivers for letting them witness it; and fear not only for the children but for the society that subjects them to the premature loss of innocence.

"Mike," Gail said, "this time we *have* to talk to the manager." We found the supervisor on duty, and she shared our feelings, but according to the law, her hands were tied: "If just one of the adults is over twenty-one," she explained, "they can bring any child they wish into these movies."

Simultaneous with this experience, I was writing *The Good Son,* a parenting plan for boys. In my research for that book, I studied thirty world cultures and found that the goal of parenting is very similar in each, even despite vast cultural differences. Parents worldwide want to raise *happy, compassionate, and self-disciplined adults.* I also discovered that in our culture, even in our efforts to raise boys this way, we are often neglectful, especially in our guidance of the often-violent, sexualized images our boys see in the media.

A decade of research into child development and the media confirms that until a child's brain develops fully, it is imprinting, modeling, and performing based on imagery it takes in from *all social sources, including the media.* Even once we're adults, our brains remain malleable to media imagery, as the continued effectiveness of commercials confirms. But among children and adolescents, the effects are even more profound. Especially until about age sixteen, the greater the exposure a boy gets to stimuli that do not teach compassion and self-restraint, the more difficult it becomes for him to learn such things. When I was growing up in the sixties, television and movies were widely beloved. Today we know that like anything we enjoy, they contain inherent dangers, too.

Over the last few years, having immersed myself in research on the effects of media on brain development, I have practiced in movie theaters what I felt was good citizenship, approaching people who brought young children into excessively violent or gory films. I've tried, without lecturing, to explain to parents the neurological and moral dangers of exposing children to this kind of developmentally dangerous stimulation. You can imagine how this has been received! I do it less now because it is hard for my wife and I to enjoy our date night when people near us are angry at my invasion of their evening. Of course, I can understand their feelings—yet if a stranger was walking up to a child on the street, harassing the boy with words and physical violence, would we not step in? How can we, in good conscience, just stand back and watch?

We can't, and yet as our culture presently has it, we are supposed to. A movie is considered outside the realm of "real" human intercourse, as is a video game, a television program, a television commercial, a CD, and so on; thus regular standards of human behavior don't apply to it. Movies are "entertainment," are not "important," so we are allowed, even encouraged, to be lax in our attitudes toward them. They are not considered to be like a stranger advancing on a child on the street, or a stranger in our homes. They are just "shows," "movies," "pictures," or "music"—somehow not real.

Yet they are all too real. As storytelling agents, media productions are as powerful as any we've ever had in history—in some neurological ways, they are even *more* powerful. To our children, who absorb life like sponges, the stories they watch and hear and read are fountains not only of entertaining stimulation but also of moral teaching about "goodness" and "badness." That is how we must know them—as our children know them.

Once we understand this, we become motivated not only to protect our children and the children around us from influences for which they are not ready, but also to redirect their energies toward stories that are actually healthy for the development of their character and happiness. Two hundred of these, in the form of books and movies, make up the body of this resource guide.

Boys Have a Special Relationship with the Media

Both girls and boys enjoy TV, pop music, video games, the Internet, movies, books, and comics. Yet *What Stories Does My Son Need?* focuses on books and movies particularly appropriate for building character and identity in boys. It lists books that will interest even the boy who doesn't like to read, and movies that will interest and challenge boys both at home and in school.

Boys have a special and highly sensitive relationship with the media. Video arcades are rarely filled with girls; nor do girls yearn as much and as stridently for their first Gameboy. Girls tend not to gravitate toward the more violent movies as often as boys do, or at as early an age. Filmmakers know that girls will go see "boy" movies but boys more rarely see "girl" movies.

The film industry produces sex-and-aggression-based programming especially to lure boys. A report by the Center for Media and Public Affairs found that while watching films, TV, and music videos, our kids absorb one scene of serious violence every four minutes. It's a visceral and hormone-driven approach to selling product. Boys are testosterone-based (testosterone is the sex and aggression hormone) and often gravitate toward stimuli that appeal to this aggression-based hormonal system.

This tends to be true all over the world. In the Indian and Chinese movie industries, for instance, sex-and-aggression programming, targeted to boys, is predominant. The world's electronic storytellers know that the male brain tends to gravitate toward fast-moving images, aggressive stimuli, flagrant sexual possibilities, and role-model males who use aggressive force. Our boys imitate these images, often verbatim.

Recently, a mother wrote me about her sons and the violent video game Apocalypse.

"I have to tell you this story about boys imitating media. One night, after playing the game, my five-year-old gave me his usual goodnight kiss, saying, 'Good night, Mom, I love you. See you in hell!' Earlier in the day I had overheard him say to his seven-year-old brother, 'Suck on this!' He's five years old! If I had ever thought before that my sons were somehow insulated from the influence of video games and TV and so on, I got a severe lesson. I threw that game away."

What is obvious in a five-year-old—imitation and modeling from the media influence—becomes subtler as the boy gets older. The male brain is forming in many ways through middle adolescence; *there is absolutely no reason to think that a boy of fifteen is immune to profound media influence.* We can be less vigilant with him, and worry less about brain-development problems in his older brain, yet he remains a growing boy.

In the end, whether the boy is five or fifteen, we simply must take control of his absorption of aggressive and sexualized media programming. Young males gravitate toward media that stimulate them to hunt and kill, as boys a thousand years ago had a special relationship with hunting and war itself. This is built into boys, to a great extent, and is enhanced by our highly violent and sex-charged culture. Boys also gravitate toward stories with role models that help them mature in all aspects of life, as they did millennia ago. Sometimes we have to be vigilant to make sure they get these role models in their reading and viewing.

Our intuition tells us our boys' exposure to unlimited and confusing media stimuli is doing harm, but how shall we regain control of the stories they hear? Movie rating systems seem to be not enough, and many media-related laws are relatively ineffective. Giving our children the right stories is not something a law will accomplish for us. We must develop higher standards among ourselves.

First, we must finally admit that the majority of media-created stories are at best *amoral*. Their purpose is obviously not to help children gain moral character and clear identity; rather, it is to sell products to children and adults, to sell actors and celebrities as products, and to imprint advertising images in our minds. Many story-creators and actors are very open about the fact that they feel little responsibility to help us build character in our children. For example, this is how Sarah Michelle Gellar, star of television's *Buffy the Vampire Slayer,* recently answered critics who pointed out that on her show a sixteen-year-old girl consistently has sex with an adult: "Lessons are to be learned from parents and teachers. Not television." We can encourage story-creators to produce moral stories, but for the sake of our children's healthy development, *we* have to pick through all the amoral products to find the real gold.

So let me suggest we do something proactive now—beyond pointing out the media's flaws—and actually covenant to take control of the stories our children experience. Let us now decide to better use the media, to which most boys are nearly addicted, to actually *build character* in boys. This is the ultimate intention of the guidebook you are reading. I hope it will help channel your boys' energy for stories beyond "entertainment," into the development of moral character and mission. I hope, too, that it will help all of us rethink the use of stories in children's lives.

Rethinking How We Use Stories

For many centuries, males were raised into manhood through the use of character- and identity-building stories, to which the adult community exposed them. In the middle ages, fairy tales, which now we read to toddlers, were in fact used to teach school-age and adolescent males the archetypal journey to maturity. During the nineteenth century, the Bible was often read and discussed at the dinner table. Stories were umbilically linked to humanity and civilization. Males learned a great deal from stories and often were "gentled" or civilized through them.

In our contemporary confusion about the worth and substance of stories—a natural confusion, given that millions of stories bombard us daily—we have forgotten their highest use. In our busy lives, we have been unable to cull the useful stories from the useless. Among all of our great-great grandparents, the most useful stories were *primal stories.*

Primal Stories

Myths and legends are primal stories, as are biblical parables, spiritual epics, many fairy tales, and some modern books and movies. These are not mere entertainment—they are *parental and communal aids for teaching the lessons of life.* They are the stories a boy *needs* in order to become a good man. In some inexplicable way, primal stories help children acccss within themselves the very power of life itself. The two hundred books and movies in this guidebook are primal stories.

Primal stories teach boys what true manhood is. One of the most significant moral questions in the human dialogue is: "What is a man?" Primal stories help answer this question. We can measure their suitability by whether they teach these ten moral competencies: *decency, fairness, empathy, self-sacrifice, responsibility, loyalty, duty, service, honesty,* and *honor.* Stories that teach these competencies are useful to our child-rearing and support children through different stages of life.

Primal stories stimulate moral dialogue—interaction between adult and child about what is compassionate, human, joy-advancing, and success-building. I hope each book and movie in this guide helps you stimulate your son to this moral dialogue. For this to occur, you and the other adults in your community must make it a part of your mission to actually take time out from the rest of life's business, and carry on this moral dialogue.

With each book or movie selected, I suggest specific ways to stimulate that dialogue—specific questions and "discussion starters" that you can use with boys. These appear at the end of each item.

I hope this book will help you revitalize the highest moral use of story in your boys' lives. I hope these books and movies will become for your family useful blueprints of the human story to be discussed between the generations. Read and view these stories as often as possible with your younger boys. Discuss them with your older boys. Watch these movies on video or DVD with your boys, and make it a family ritual to morally debate the substance of the story presented. Help your sons discover the role models, and the worth of those models, in each story. Sophocles said, "It is by the story that you know the soul." The soul of each boy is inspired by primal stories that make him see himself, as if in the hidden mirror of all humanity.

A Word of Thanks

As I prepared to write this book, I realized I needed another mind to join me in finding just the right movies and books. It is a major responsibility to set out to delineate two hundred books and movies that boys *need*. Terry Trueman, whom I've known for almost two decades, is not only an accomplished writer, movie critic, and longtime teacher but also the father of two sons. I want to thank him for his help and make special note of something he has taught me: "No matter what you do with a list like this, people are going to disagree with you!"

I hope, as you read and utilize this book, that you will forgive us for any choices that you think are inappropriate. If you have any concerns or suggestions, I hope you'll write us at the address in the back of this book. You may find yourself thinking, as one parent wrote me about the similar, smaller list I included in *The Good Son:* "How can you suggest the movie *He Got Game* for an eighth grader? It's filled with immoral actions." After listening to this parent's arguments, I ended up agreeing that this film should be removed.

Books and movies are very intimate and personal things, so my selection of primal stories may include elements that others just won't like. But I hope, as you apply your family's and community's standards, you'll allow some latitude. The Bible, like so many other sacred moral texts, is itself filled with violence, adultery, and many elements that we don't want our kids imitating—and yet at the center of the biblical story (or Bhagavad Gita or Koran or Zen tales) is the primal story of human development, which all of our children need to experience.

Tips for Making This Book Work for You

This guide contains two sections, one for movies, one for books. Each section is divided into four parts:

> Preschool/Kindergarten
>
> Elementary School
> > Lower Grades 1–3
> > Upper Grades 4–6
>
> Middle School
>
> High School

In my placement especially of movies, I am generally protective—some might say overprotective. I place a movie in the age category in which a boy will surely understand it (sometimes with your interpretive help) and not be harmed by it. Your intuition will, of course, be better than mine at determining whether your own child can handle a movie I've placed within his age group. On a few occasions, you may encounter a movie that you feel you must protect him from. I hope you'll consider my list only a start, not an ultimate statement. The most difficult age-span to place is the elementary school age. There is a great diversity between what a first and fifth grader can handle. I hope that if your boy is in this group, you'll be particularly careful with my choices.

As you use this book, you may often be challenged by your son's plea, "You don't have to watch a movie with me. You don't have to pick movies for me—I'm old enough to do it." Quite often, he is old enough; but just as often, he's not. Especially for an elementary-school-age boy, it is essential to choose, view, or read stories with him. On the other hand, with a middle teen, you can often only suggest he watch or read something, and then hope he'll dialogue with you about it.

It helps if you set up a ritual time to watch or read the primal movies and books in the family. If you start doing this while your son is young, even the middle teen will still look forward to family movie time together.

Our boys are beautiful souls often adrift in a culture of

overstimulation. They want to know the hidden life story, but their male identities become fragmented parts of a million pseudostories. May this guide help you bring order to some of the frenzy of images in your son's world.

In so doing, I hope you and I together will rethink childhood itself, one story at a time.

100
MOVIES

Preschool/ Kindergarten

BABE (1995)

Children adore the wonderful world of Babe, a pig who refuses to believe that she can't do the job of a ranch dog. In Babe's world, animals talk—special effects make their lips move in perfect pronunciation of sounds, from fricatives to trills—and a dog (or a pig, for that matter) is valued according to how hard he works. *Babe* wonderfully teaches boys that love and belief in oneself can overcome great odds and apparent handicaps.

Discussion Starters: *What is your favorite thing about how Babe treats the other animals? Why do the sheep finally decide to cooperate with Babe? What does this story say about how we should treat animals?*

BAMBI (1942)

This animated classic, one of the first and greatest of Disney's many anthropomorphizing films, presents the life of a deer from birth to adulthood. A metaphor for all boys growing up, *Bambi* does what all great stories make us do: both laugh and cry. The lessons of life and character taught by this wonderful story are value-rich: courage, sacrifice, nobility, honor, fairness, and a deep abiding love and respect for nature.

Discussion Starters: *In what ways is Bambi like you? At the end of the story, who is Bambi most like? What scares Bambi? Does that same thing scare you sometimes?*

BEAUTY AND THE BEAST (1991)

This magical, mythological tale is about the saving power of love. Beauty, a sweet and kind young woman, is held at the castle of the brooding, dark, and mysterious Beast. The result is a wonderful lesson in seeing through appearances, learning to control impulses, discovering what real men and women are, and committing ourselves to love. Watching this video, children feel that anyone who is willing and able to love will be loved in return, and that feeling love will transform and change them forever. This animated version is wonderful not only for younger children but for adults as well.

Discussion Starters: *When people say they love you, do*

you like yourself even more? Is it more important to be pretty or brave? How is Beauty just as brave as the Beast?

FREE WILLY (1993)

A lonely boy makes a friend—a two-ton killer whale! An unusual boy/animal pairing, this marvelous film teaches our sons that they will inherit a planet where concern for nature is not an abstract option but a moral imperative. *Free Willy* is a boy's struggle to set free and thereby *lose* the thing he loves most. Loving, thus, is sometimes about putting the person or thing we love ahead of ourselves—a painful but necessary character lesson.

Discussion Starters: *Why does Jesse have to let Willy go free? Even when you are apart from someone, can you still love them just as much? What does Jesse learn about friendship from Willy?*

THE IRON GIANT (1999)

A boy stumbles upon a giant made of iron who fell from the sky. While he is mentored by a sculptor and hounded by an obsessive government agent, the boy shows immense compassion toward his large but unworldly and confused friend. In the end, the iron giant must sacrifice himself to save his friends, a heart-wrenching and very meaningful experience for both the boy and the viewing audience. This is a beautiful moral tale, set in 1950s America.

Discussion Starters: *Why does the giant have to be blown up in the end? Is there a bad guy in this movie, or is everyone trying to do what he considers to be right?*

LASSIE COME HOME (1943)

Often boys learn early lessons about responsibility through their relationships with their pets, especially dogs. *Lassie Come Home,* in this classic version, shows how love and commitment can overcome amazing obstacles. Faithful to the novel *Lassie Come Home,* this first great Lassie movie is a priceless teaching tool to inspire a boy's sense of duty.

Discussion Starters: *Is this movie a "love story"? If you could, would you want to have a friend like Lassie? What responsibilities go with owning a pet?*

THE LION KING (1994)

This animated Disney movie tells the story of a lion "prince" who loses his father and flees, believing that his father's death was his own fault. Befriended by a hog and a muskrat, and inspired to become a moral and compassionate adult, the prince returns home, becomes the king, and brings his beleaguered kingdom to prosperity. This movie is good for late toddlers and school-age children, and it is even useful in high school ethics curricula.

Discussion Starters: *Why does the little lion cub believe that it's his fault that his father died? How does the evil uncle, Scar,*

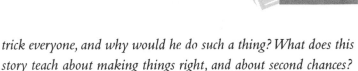

trick everyone, and why would he do such a thing? What does this story teach about making things right, and about second chances?

MIRACLE ON 34TH STREET (1947, 1994)

In many families, viewing one version of this movie is an annual Christmas tradition (along with *It's a Wonderful Life;* see page 27). Both versions are good and are good places to start a conversation about the "real meaning of Christmas," which must explain that giving and receiving gifts can and should be a gesture in giving and receiving love. This story teaches that even for confused adults, goodwill and caring are all around us, if only we all keep our faith and truly believe.

Discussion Starters: *How does Kris prove to everyone that he is really Santa Claus? Explain how magic and miracles happen every day (hint: sunrises, sunsets, a spider's web, a summer rain). This Christmas, what would someone else like to receive for a present?*

MULAN (1998)

This animated film tells the story of a girl who must dress up as a young man in order to save her family's honor and prove herself. It is funny, filled with adventure, and exciting for both boys and girls. Young boys take to it as much as girls, learning about duty, hard work, telling the truth, doing your best, loving your family, and growing up.

Discussion Starters: *What does this story teach you about responsibility and working hard? What does the word* honor *mean? Shouldn't boys and girls both be given the same chances in life to do the best they can do?*

PETER PAN (1953)

There have been many film versions of this story (including Steven Spielberg's 1991 *Hook*), but the Disney animated version is still the classic. The Peter Pan stories teach boys that it takes great courage to be a child and equally great courage to face the responsibilities of growing up. Certainly, while every kid must grow up, the best adults retain a little bit of the child in them.

Discussion Starters: *Peter Pan never wants to grow up—can you see why? Never Never Land is far away, but can you go there in your imagination? Talk about other ways to "fly," as in the flight of the imagination.*

PINOCCHIO (1940)

"Always let your conscience be your guide." Whether a boy hears this sentiment from Polonius in Shakespeare's *Hamlet* or from Jiminy Cricket in *Pinocchio,* the message is a crucial one. The little wooden boy Pinocchio sometimes forgets Jiminy's wise words, with fairly awful consequences, which will inspire your son to learn from his mistakes and strive for high standards of honor. This Disney animated feature version is a terrific film, as good today as it was when it premiered in 1940.

Discussion Starters: *In real life, does your nose grow when you tell a lie? If not, then why is it wrong to lie? How does Pinocchio "earn" the right to become a real boy?*

THE PRINCE OF EGYPT (1998)

A retelling of the Moses story, this animated version takes some liberties with biblical events yet retains the original substance of the story, with powerful results. Children and adults who view this movie together will be moved by the journey of Moses from spirited boy to spiritually mature man, and they will share his pain at being an agent of destruction to the Egyptians, who are, in essence, his friends and family. This film inspires compassion in little boys in beautiful ways.

Discussion Starters: *Why wouldn't the pharaoh let Moses' people go? How do you think you would feel if you had to hurt your friends because you knew it was right to do so—for instance, if you had to tell on a friend who was doing something very wrong?*

SWISS FAMILY ROBINSON (1960)

A close, loving family becomes stranded on a tropical island and uses its ingenuity to make the best of it (building, while they're at it, the most amazing treehouse ever). Their tropical paradise is interrupted by the arrival of pirates, and eventually a great battle between the family and the evil intruders unfolds. Even the youngest children can understand the idealistic yet reassuring moral to this story: that a good and loving family, by working and sticking together, can make a wonderful, happy life in any circumstances.

Discussion Starters: *What does this story teach about loyalty within a family and the importance of working together? How does this family's willingness to respect one another and work hard together help save them?*

THE SWORD IN THE STONE (1963)

The ancient tale of King Arthur as a boy is both exciting and moving, as the young Arthur overcomes many obstacles on his journey not just to adulthood but to leadership and legend. Some of the relationships and "magic" may need explanation for younger viewers, but once they grasp the basics, this animated movie is one that little boys often love to watch over and over again. They learn that any boy with enough faith in himself and enough courage can prove what real nobility is really all about.

Discussion Starters: *How does Merlin the magician help young Wart to become a great king named Arthur? What does Merlin teach Wart by changing him into different kinds of animals? If you were a king, what would you do to make the world a better place?*

Elementary School

Lower Grades 1-3

CAPTAINS COURAGEOUS (1937)

The Academy Award–winning performance by Spencer Tracy as Manuel, a Portuguese fisherman, is part of what explains this film's enduring popularity. But Freddie Bartholomew is equally compelling as the spoiled son of a wealthy tycoon. These two lead characters meet when the boy falls off a passenger ship and is pulled from the water by Manuel. Although their relationship is a little rough at the beginning, it is one of growing respect and friendship and a marvelous model of mentoring. (See *Scent of a Woman,* page 74, for another.) Boys learn that in loving and raising a child, time, attention, and responsibility are more important than material well-being.

Discussion Starters: *How was the boy spoiled and selfish in the early parts of this film? Why does Manuel love his own father so much? What does this story show you about hard work and self-esteem?*

COOL RUNNINGS (1993)

When the tropical island nation of Jamaica (whose tourist motto might as well be "Never Had Any Snow, Never Will") announced that it intended to enter a bobsled team in the 1988 Winter Olympics, everyone laughed. But the moral of this funny, sweet, inspirational little story, based on true events, testifies to sportsmanship, teamwork, competition, and most of all, the importance of living out one's dreams.

Discussion Starters: *Why is "follow your dream" an important message? What does this film teach about never giving up? Even though they come in last, why are these Jamaican bobsledders the biggest "winners" of all?*

E.T.: THE EXTRA-TERRESTRIAL (1982)

Elliot is a boy whose family is facing emotional difficulties. When he first meets E.T., both are in desperate need of a friend. This wonderful film depicts how a boy transcends his loneliness to care about others, regardless of how different they are from him. Elliot's adventure helps him, and every boy, learn to care about and love himself.

Discussion Starters: *Elliot and E.T. learn to understand each other's feelings—discuss how this is the meaning of empathy. Just because E.T. has to fly away, that doesn't mean that he and Elliot aren't friends; discuss how real friends are close even when far apart geographically. Why do the government agents think they are right to try to capture E.T.?*

IT'S A WONDERFUL LIFE (1946)

The hero of this Christmas classic doesn't realize his own worth until it's almost too late. I've watched the film with young men, only to find all of our eyes brimming with tears. It is an important film about family, courage, and character. While appropriate for little boys, it is useful also with young adults.

Discussion Starters: *How does the angel show Bailey that his life has been important? Talk about the people in your life who have, without even knowing it, made a huge difference.*

OLD YELLER (1957)

Two brothers on a Texas farm teach a mutt with bad manners how to be great dog. The dog, in turn, teaches the boys, especially the older one (played by Tommy Kirk), about friendship and loyalty. No one can watch the conclusion of Old Yeller without shedding tears. The important moral of the story lies in the sad, hard conclusion: that there are always costs to loving, and sometimes a heavy, heartbreaking price to pay (see also *The Red Pony,* page 117), yet one worth paying.

Discussion Starters: *In what scene do the boys and the dog first become aware of how much they mean to one another? Why does Old Yeller have to be destroyed in the end? Have you ever had a favorite pet die? If so, talk about it.*

THE PRIDE OF THE YANKEES (1942)

Based on the life of Lou Gehrig, this classic baseball movie may strike some as a little dated and corny, but its core values—modesty, pride, hard work, and overcoming the struggle between devotion to family and dreams—are timeless and essential. Gary Cooper plays Gehrig, one of the greatest ballplayers of all time on the greatest team ever (the Yankees of the late 1920s and early 1930s). During his career, playing in the enormous shadow of Babe Ruth, Gehrig was considered only a "very good" ballplayer. Only after he became sick and had to end his streak of two thousand–plus games (a record that stood for over thirty years) was his true value both to his team and to the game fully appreciated. Gehrig's astonishing work ethic was a living metaphor of responsibility and duty.

Discussion Starters: *Why don't Lou's parents want him to be a baseball player? Why is Lou's record of consecutive starts so*

amazing? Why does Lou call himself the "luckiest man alive," even though he is dying of a terrible disease?

THE PRINCESS BRIDE (1987)

A grandfather, played touchingly by Peter Falk, sits down to read a story to his grandson, who is home from school with a bad cold. The grandson is reluctant to hear it because it's titled *The Princess Bride,* not very promising for a ten-year-old boy. Yet what transpires over the next hundred or so minutes is an amazing and wonderful viewing experience for boys. It shows our sons what is truly important in life—true love—and what sacrifices we must make for it.

Discussion Starters: *How is young Westley transformed into the "dread Pirate Robert"? What does the story show about teamwork? When the grandfather says to his grandson "As you wish," what is he really saying?*

SHANE (1953)

Alan Ladd plays a quiet loner named Shane who shows up in a small ranching community in the rugged, violent Old West. He is an honest, trustworthy, hard-working, and independent man—a powerful role model for boys, who learn from him honesty, courage, and faith in oneself. His friendship with the boy in this classic film touches everyone, adult or child.

Discussion Starters: *Why is Shane trying so hard to avoid violence? In the scene where Shane and his friend work at pulling the stump out of the ground, what did you learn about friendship, hard work, and victory? In the gunfight, would Shane have had to kill the "bad" guys if there had been honest policemen and enforceable laws?*

TREASURE ISLAND (1990)

There are three terrific film versions of Robert Louis Stevenson's story about treasure and pirates, but the 1990 television production, starring Charlton Heston as Long John Silver, is especially dynamic. For younger children, you might consider the simpler 1950 Disney version. Whichever production you choose, you won't be disappointed, nor will your son, and the message of the story remains as valuable as ever: that dreams of great wealth always end up costing more than you expect, so know your own worth from inside yourself, not from what you can hoard.

Discussion Starters: *Why is Long John Silver such an unforgettable character? If you found a treasure map, what would you do? If you had a huge amount of money, would it make you happy?*

WHERE THE RED FERN GROWS (1974)

Set in Oklahoma during the Great Depression, *Where the Red Fern Grows* is a deeply affecting picture of a young man

coming of age as he accepts responsibility for the care and training of his beloved hunting dogs. This film has an old-fashioned, Norman Rockwell feel to it, showing, in often touching detail, a boy who gains the ability to sacrifice and care about others.

Discussion Starters: *Why is it so important to train the dogs to hunt well? How are these dogs different from just "pets"? What part of this story makes you happiest? Saddest? Explain.*

WILLOW (1998)

Few films show people who live with dwarfism in interesting and significant roles. Not only does *Willow* do this, but it casts a dwarf actor as the protagonist and hero. This alone makes *Willow* a good film for opening an important dialogue with boys about the nature of "handicaps," "disabilities," and being just plain "being different." The film spins a great yarn of heroes saving their people. Full of magic and the triumph of good over evil, it shows that courage, heroism and strength are *not* dependent on the size of the package in which they come.

Discussion Starters: *What does this story tell us about the real meaning of stature? How does Willow make up for his size with his intelligence and courage? What does the expression "you can't judge a book by its cover" mean?*

Upper Grades 4–6

THE BEAR (1989)

This gracefully filmed story by French filmmaker Jean-Jacques Annaud rises above the genre of "animal movies" to present a poignant and affecting story about nature, honor, courage, and strength. The bad guys are men with guns, while the heroes are a bear and a cub. There is no dialogue in this film, yet it is an amazing achievement. Its best lesson is wrapped up in a single and unforgettable scene by a waterfall, where one of the hunters, trapped and at the bear's mercy, learns compassion. The bear doesn't use words for this lecture, but the human most certainly gets the message!

Discussion Starters: *What does this story show about the environment and man's relationship to other creatures? How does the bear prove that he is more moral and better than the men are? How and why is the one man changed by his experiences with the bear?*

BEETHOVEN LIVES UPSTAIRS (1989)

This made-for-TV movie is about Beethoven as a mentorial boarder in a ten-year-old boy's house. Music and the arts constantly provide a backdrop for the boy's development of self-discipline and self-worth. This film captures a boy's relationship with music, with a mentor, and with life's lessons.

Discussion Starters: *If you could pick any figure from history to be your mentor, who would it be and why? Who are the mentors in your life? What values do you learn from them?*

THE BLACK STALLION (1979)

Based on the wonderful children's novel by Walter Farley, this film depicts a boy's life on a deserted island with no one but a wild black horse to keep him company. Directed by Caroll Ballard, who also filmed the equally graceful *Never Cry Wolf* (page 37), this is a story about a boy who learns, through a connection with a living thing, responsibility and how to love.

Discussion Starters: *How does the boy start to win the horse's trust? Talk about the word* transition *as it applies to the boy's efforts to readjust to "civilized" life again. How does the relationship between the boy and the trainer (played by Mickey Rooney) help the boy and the horse to grow even closer?*

BRIAN'S SONG (1971)

This is a moving story of life lived to the fullest: of competition, empathy, friendship, and death's power. It is most suitable for boys ten and older. When the quiet, introverted pro football player Gale Sayers (played by Billy Dee Williams) stands up to deliver a eulogy to his fallen teammate Brian Piccolo (played by James Caan), it is difficult for any boy to resist tears. Throughout the film, boys sense how love between friends can grow even when the friends are very different. Finally, they see that losing a friend to death makes sense only when we remember all that we once shared in life. This film might find a special place in the life of a boy who has recently lost a relative or friend.

Discussion Starters: *How do Sayers's and Piccolo's differences help to bring them closer? Why does Brian push Gale so hard during Gale's rehabilitation from the injured knee? Why is it so moving when Gale says, "I loved Brian Piccolo," and why is it so important to tell your friends how you feel about them?*

EMPIRE OF THE SUN (1987)

Based on a true story, this survival tale, in the capable hands of Steven Spielberg, shows a child's-eye view of the horrors of war. An underrated film, it contains many moments of touching beauty and poignant fear, as a ten-year-old boy learns what it takes to survive, both physically and spiritually, in war-torn Asia during World War II. No child should ever have to endure what the young boy did, but the film is an excellent teaching tool for reaching children from chaotic/dysfunctional backgrounds. After watching what this boy survives, one understands that hope, faith, and courage are indispensable for enduring hard times.

Discussion Starters: *Can you imagine suddenly being in a situation where only your own wits can save you? What does the hero learn about survival in this story? If the Japanese had won*

World War II, do you think Ballard would still, one day, have found his way back to his family again?

FORREST GUMP (1994)

"I'm a simple man, but I know what love is," says the protagonist of this remarkable film starring Tom Hanks. A haunting story, *Forrest Gump* shows that intelligence is sometimes less important than love, honor, self-respect, courage, and kindness.

Discussion Starters: *In what ways is Jenny more "handicapped" than Forrest? What does Forrest's mom mean when she says, "Stupid is as stupid does"? Forrest says he knows what love is—do you? Give a definition of being loved and loving others.*

THE GODS MUST BE CRAZY (1980)

This odd, whimsical film about a tribal man whose adventures bring him into contact with Western civilization teaches our sons how cultures meet and bungle their meetings but still find common ground. In the end, values such as service, self-sacrifice, fairness, and decency are universal to all people in all cultures.

Discussion Starters: *How do the "primitive" people seem to live more comfortably than those of us living in "civilized" societies? What objects are sacred to you in your culture? How far would you go to protect them?*

IRON WILL (1994)

This is the story of a young man who enters a grueling dogsled race in an effort to save his family's farm and raise money to go to college. A coming-of-age film set at the very cusp of a boy's transition into manhood, *Iron Will* illustrates how character is forged through hardship and the exercise of fairness, courage, and discipline.

Discussion Starters: *Would you do what Will did if your family was in the position his was? How does Will's relationship with his dogs pay off in the end? When bad guys in your life act as bad as the bad guys in this story did, what should you do?*

THE KARATE KID (1984)

Unabashed in its Cinderella-like theme, this family classic of a boy who trains in the martial arts provides a model of self-transformation through hard work and perseverance, particularly with the crucial guiding hand of a beloved mentor. In practical terms, it reminds us that martial arts and mentorship are beneficial to any boy who is either being bullied or is unable to control his own aggressive urges.

Discussion Starters: *How does "wax on—wax off" teach and build strength in Daniel? What does this story teach about fairness and honor? What is wrong with trying to win at all costs?*

MY BODYGUARD (1980)

In this film about bullying and pecking orders, a smart undersized kid "hires" a brooding oversized kid to protect him from a gang of school extortionists—in other words, to be his bodyguard. The film shows the deep sensitivity and pain that lie under the surface of a "tough guy," the inevitability and importance of fighting one's own battles, and the fact that while friendships can start in a variety of ways, they grow through kindness and caring.

Discussion Starters: *This film was made in an era where losing a fistfight did not mean that the loser returned the next day with a gun for revenge—is the world different now? As enjoyable as it is to see the mean bully finally get his comeuppance, are there other ways to handle these kinds of problems? Would it have been a better idea to press charges against the bullies for theft and then let the police handle the matter?*

NEVER CRY WOLF (1983)

A biologist goes up to the Arctic, alone, to study the social lives, habits, and ways of wolves in the wild—and learns even more about himself, nature, and the quest for meaning and compassion. This story, better than many others that try to force a message, teaches that we all have more to gain by pursuing a course of empathy and love than by assuming antagonistic relationships.

Discussion Starters: *Can you imagine being alone in the* *wild for many months? What would you do? What does the title mean? How does it apply to this movie, and to you?*

RUDY (1993)

Rudy decides, at the age of ten, that the only thing that matters in life is to play football for the University of Notre Dame. A wonderful film for teaching boys about focus, sacrifice, goal setting, loyalty, and believing in yourself despite the odds, it inspires an attitude toward life that can't be given, only earned.

Discussion Starters: *Why is it so important to Rudy to play football for Notre Dame? Is anything in your life that important to you? Do you think all of Rudy's sacrifices were worthwhile in the end?*

SCROOGED (1988)

This humorous Christmas morality play tells the story of a warped TV executive who learns the meaning of compassion. Especially at the Christmas season, this film is good for both home and school. While Charles Dickens's *A Christmas Carol* has been filmed many times and carries an original moral theme, older boys sometimes find the straight story boring. They won't find Bill Murray's *Scrooged* anything but fun.

Discussion Starters: *Why does the Ghost of Christmas*

Present visit? What does this movie say about the real "meaning" of Christmas?

SIMON BIRCH (1996)

This film tells the story of a disabled boy who seems to intrinsically understand the real meaning of self-sacrifice. He is humiliated by society but has an inborn sense of character that inspires not only the children and adults in his community but all of us who watch him try to save his friends.

Discussion Starters: *How is Simon much, much more than the sum of his small parts? What does this story teach about the idea of "handicap"?*

THE SOUND OF MUSIC (1965)

The Sound of Music is a classic not just because of its music and action but because of its moral center. In the face of evil, in this case Nazism, a family decides to sacrifice all—an important message both historically and perpetually.

Discussion Starters: *How does Maria win over the children? Explain how difficult it would be to make the decision the family makes, even though in hindsight it seems easy now. How have you had to make important sacrifices in your life?*

THE TEN COMMANDMENTS (1956)

Filmed almost half a century ago, this relatively long film has held up remarkably well, inspiring generations of children to higher purposes. Charlton Heston's Moses teaches unforgettable lessons about dedication, responsibility, and duty.

Discussion Starters: *Explain the history of the Jews and the biblical character of Moses. What are the Ten Commandments, and why are they still good rules to go by? Why would God, who supposedly loves everyone, let the sea fall on all those Egyptians? (This question will help start a discussion about the bad things that happen in life and God's role in the universe.)*

THREE WISHES (1995)

Two boys and a single mom are struggling when a mysterious man enters their lives. He teaches the boys what it means to endure and to discover personal self-confidence. Because it involves boys' loneliness for their dad, who has disappeared, many boys who are facing their own father's absence may find it especially inspiring.

Discussion Starters: *Take a minute to think—what would be your greatest wish? Explain. What can you do to feel better when you know you can't control events around you? What "wish" does the boy get once he becomes a man?*

TO KILL A MOCKINGBIRD (1962)

A stirring condemnation of prejudice and the ignorance required for it to flourish, this story (see "100 Books," page 136) has important social themes that still hold relevance today. We are hard-pressed to imagine a more admirable role model than Atticus Finch, played by Gregory Peck, be it as father, attorney, or community leader. Atticus knows to the depths of his being that doing the right thing, regardless of the costs, is always necessary and correct.

Discussion Starters: *How does Scout "grow up" during the time this story takes place? Have you had to take a stand yet in your life as Atticus did? Has anyone else you know? Explain why you think Atticus's belief in the law is such an important value to him.*

WARGAMES (1983)

Matthew Broderick plays a precocious teenager who inadvertently breaks into a major military computer system and, thinking it's a game, sets off a chain of events that could lead to an unprecedented disaster. Implausible? Absolutely. Impossible? We all wish it were, but we know better. *Wargames* shows us that simply *saying* "I take full responsibility" is only a first step toward righting a wrong. A man must actually take responsibility and set things right again. This film ends with the prophetic message that sometimes the only way to "win" is not to play at all.

Discussion Starters: *Why do you think the world's great powers built so many weapons of mass destruction in the first place? How does the game of tic-tac-toe "teach" the computer that "mutual assured global destruction" is a "no-win game"?*

Middle School

APOLLO 13 (1995)

Apollo 13 makes it clear that scientists are much more than just nerds. This powerful story shows how individuals use their intelligence, education, and dedication to solve a problem that saves lives while at the same time exploring the galaxy. Brimming with images of self-sacrifice, honor, faith, and service, this film helps instill maturity and also, like *The Edge* (page 65), shows the powerful relationship between one's values and one's behavior in times of stress and crisis.

Discussion Starters: *When people jokingly say, "You don't have to be a rocket scientist to figure such and such . . . ," what do they mean? Explain how this film portrays the success of the*

American space program as resulting from a team approach to solving problems. What qualities of character do you think you'd need to be an astronaut?

BEN-HUR (1959)

This classic is a story of Jesus Christ told from the perspective of a man named Ben-Hur, who lives in the same era as Jesus. In some ways, Ben-Hur's torments, struggles, and triumphs mirror Christ's life—several times the two men even meet. Ben-Hur learns, after enormous pain and hardship, that peace begins and ends in the human heart. Because this film is long (211 minutes), it's often best for boys to view it in segments.

    Discussion Starters: *When Ben-Hur's friend turns against him, how is this betrayal worse than he could have imagined? In the end, how does the message of this story, like the message of Christianity itself, suggest that the most important things in life are bigger than the time or place where one lives?*

THE BRIDGE ON THE RIVER KWAI (1957)

This classic film about the conflict between duty to self and duty to others shows honor and courage as values present on both sides of a war. Alec Guinness plays the commander of a group of British and American prisoners of war who are being forced to build a bridge for their Japanese captors. In the midst of its gripping portrait of three very different cultures, this film depicts the universality of a man's struggle to maintain meaning and humanity during the senseless inhumanity of war.

Discussion Starters: *Does this story help you see how important it is to keep your duties clear in your mind no matter where you are? What does this film say about loyalty to yourself, to your own values and honor? In the end, how does blowing up the bridge make just as much sense as building it did?*

CHARIOTS OF FIRE (1981)

When should a man's conscience and sense of religious duty take priority over his personal ambition? This celebrated film answers this question. Few movies capture so fully the nobility of men found in competitiveness, and the hidden truth that every man must learn: Some things in life are more important than winning.

Discussion Starters: *Why does one runner feel that it is not right to run on a Sunday? How is the competition between the "world's fastest runners" shown to be fierce but respectful? In the end, why isn't winning the most important thing?*

THE COLOR PURPLE (1985)

Based on Alice Walker's Pulitzer Prize—winning novel of life in the poor South, *The Color Purple* tells a story of survival—spiritual as well as physical—amid cruelty and poverty, and of the terrible price that individuals and families pay for freedom. This troubling film will definitely require discussion, but it is an important one in a boy's development of moral clarity.

Discussion Starters: *Is Mister (Danny Glover's character) evil, or is he just ignorant and selfish? How does this film show that the times are changing greatly, as are the characters? What is the most important difference between the African characters and the African-Americans who are their relatives, in terms of pride, confidence, and self-assurance?*

DANCES WITH WOLVES (1990)

At the beginning of this film, Lieutenant John Dunbar lies on an operating table in a military field hospital during the American Civil War. Through his pain he hears the surgeons deciding to have some coffee before they amputate his badly wounded foot. Dunbar rises from his cot and rides into moral fable, myth, and legend. His new life, among the tribe of Indians he meets and joins, is a deeply compelling and moving story of a man who has the character to understand himself, act fairly, and lead other human beings through pain and peril.

Discussion Starters: *How does the change in the way Dunbar wears his uniform show how he is changing? What things seem "better" about the Indians' way of life? Do you think that this*

story shows some of the reasons why America's treatment of Indians was unfair and tragic? If so, explain.

DEAD POETS SOCIETY (1989)

An unconventional teacher mentors boys at a strict boarding school in a film that captures the beauty and the grief that male friendship can carry. As the boys find the opportunity to be good young men, they also discover the freedom to make critical mistakes, and experience the consequences. This is a tough film, dealing with some mature themes; thus it is suitable for older middle school and most high school audiences.

Discussion Starters: *Does Mr. Keating give his students too much hope and freedom? What does it mean when the boys stand on their chairs at the end? Why does Neil take his own life?*

EDWARD SCISSORHANDS (1990)

With the surreal sensibility of a primal fable, *Edward Scissorhands* is an allegory for every boy who has ever felt that he doesn't quite fit in. The message is that sometimes love cannot conquer all but that other character qualities—self-sacrifice, honor, decency, and kindness—can.

Discussion Starters: *How does this movie teach the value of judging people by their heart rather than by their appearance? Why is this value* always *important to remember?*

THE ELEPHANT MAN (1980)

When this film was originally released, the advertisements refused to show the title character in anything but silhouette. If you wanted to "see" the elephant man, you had to pay your admission. Ironically, this is exactly what happened to the real John Merrick, the elephant man, about whom this amazing film was made. Because of a horrifying birth defect, Merrick's head, back, and one arm were grotesquely disfigured. This film shows how horribly he was treated— exploited as a circus freak—and how he overcame it to find for himself a place of dignity, honor, and nobility. A story of astonishing cruelty, courage, and somehow genuine beauty, *The Elephant Man* teaches that the human spirit is capable of overcoming virtually any obstacle. It may be difficult for less mature middle school viewers.

Discussion Starters: *Why is it especially cruel to call John Merrick an "elephant man"? What is Merrick saying when he yells at the gawking people "I am not an animal, I am a human being"? What does the pretty actress mean when she tells Merrick that he is "beautiful"?*

FIELD OF DREAMS (1989)

"If you build it, they will come," whispers a voice in the wind—never quite explaining what "it" is or who "they" are. Part sports fantasy, part familial allegory, and part mythical tale, this film is a wonderful vehicle for understanding the humanity and frailty of the father-son relationship. Through that understanding, so many of life's basic lessons become clear.

Discussion Starters: *Explain why some people see Ray's building of the baseball diamond as "crazy." How does this film show the values of self-sacrifice, love, and responsibility? Have you noticed how difficult it is sometimes for men to connect emotionally with each other?*

GANDHI (1982)

In this epic film, Ben Kingsley plays the saintly leader of India's successful nonviolent revolution for independence against the British. Especially valuable for young American male viewers is the revelation of how one man's belief and dedication to his principles changed the world. Diversity, antiracism, and cultural awareness are merely side benefits of this story about how tolerance, courage, and discipline, not violence or war, made the world a different and better place.

Discussion Starters: *Gandhi wears "traditional" clothes made from "homespun" cloth—explain why. What do you think Gandhi means when he says that he always forgives sinners because he has sinned so much himself? If you could meet Gandhi, what would you say to him or ask him?*

GLORY (1989)

Our boys are hungry to learn how to value their own individual worth against larger social backdrops. *Glory* provides a life-defining story of principles, ideas, and values worth dying for, set against the backdrop of the Civil War. It shows that patriotism is not the same as jingoism. Like *Braveheart* (page 61), it inspires crucial discussion of personal freedom, one of humanity's greatest and most important values.

Discussion Starters: *What do you make of how, at one point in American history, the gift of freedom was denied to a significant percentage of our population because of the pigmentation of their skin? Explain how this is one of our greatest legacies of shame.*

THE GRAPES OF WRATH (1940)

The Grapes of Wrath (see "100 Books," page 109) is unparalleled in its ability to teach our sons lessons of family love and spiritual struggle, as it tells the tragic story of the Joad family's struggle to survive during the Dust Bowl era of the Great Depression. Few stories could better prepare boys for the kinds of strength and values they will need when they have to endure their own "hard times." This movie is most comprehensible when accompanied by a brief history lesson in the Dust Bowl.

Discussion Starters: *Have you ever gone to bed at night* *hungry, with no idea when you'll have something to eat again? If not, how do you think that would feel? Is true wealth having millions of dollars, or is it just the security of knowing that you can take care of yourself and your loved ones? Ask your grandparents what it was like during the Great Depression, or read more about it, and remark on what you have learned.*

HIGH NOON (1952)

In this Western classic, a lone sheriff displays matchless courage when a freed convict seeks to hunt him down. For boys who must face down a bully, this movie may be of special inspiration. It also shows how we must sometimes fight our own battles, without the support of friends.

Discussion Starters: *What does this film teach you about honor? What is honor? How does Gary Cooper's character put duty and responsibility first? Are there less violent ways that one can show the same kind of courage, such as owning up to making a mistake and accepting responsibility for it?*

HOOSIERS (1986)

Like many other sports-oriented films (*Breaking Away* and *Rudy*), *Hoosiers* depicts young men struggling to develop character, discipline, and courage against the backdrop of athletics, in this case a basketball team seeking a championship. It is suitable for most middle and high school boys, and some late-elementary-school-age boys.

Discussion Starters: *Why was it so important for the boys to listen to their coach? Should the coach have been given a second chance? Why is it so amazing that the town of Hickory wins the championship?*

LUCAS (1986)

In many ways, Lucas is the quintessential nerd, the kind of kid who defends himself against insults by showing the bullies that he's smarter than they are. This is often not a great strategy for adolescent survival, but Lucas does survive, and his sense of fairness, decency, and loyalty gives boys who see themselves as nerdy a terrific role model. A wonderful story for your pubescent son, during that time in his life when he feels awkward and unlovable and only his feet seem to be growing, Lucas is ultimately a lesson in self-respect.

Discussion Starters: *What are your true talents? Are you doing everything you can to develop them? Why do some of the kids pick on Lucas so much? Lucas earns respect the hard way; can you think of other ways he might have earned that respect?*

MASK (1985)

Like *The Elephant Man* (see page 48), *Mask* tells the true story of a person overcoming a deforming disease. Eric Stoltz plays Rocky, the teenage victim of a birth defect that has disfigured him, especially in the head and face. Unlike the nineteenth-century John Merrick, Rocky lives through

this experience in modern America. All teens, at times, feel ugly and worry about their appearance. *Mask* may not resolve such feelings, but it shows that looks are not the most important thing, and it inspires boys to focus on their own moral centers more than on social conventions.

Discussion Starters: *How much value do you put on how you look? Does watching* Mask *help you realize that your appearance is* not *the most important thing about you? Can you think of ways in which Rocky is luckier than a lot of other kids?*

MEN DON'T LEAVE (1990)

A father dies, and a mother (movingly played by Jessica Lange) and her two teenage sons must find a way to cope. A powerful depiction of the relationship between a single mother and her boys, this film challenges middle school and older boys to understand loyalty, family love, and how hard they have to work to become responsible men.

Discussion Starters: *Are there ways you could help your family to be stronger? What does this film teach you about a mother's love?*

MR. HOLLAND'S OPUS (1996)

This long, rewarding film follows the life of a high school music teacher, Glenn Holland, his family, and the school to which he gives so much of his life. Mr. Holland, who loves music with a great and abiding passion, learns that he loves teaching to a similar degree and accepts, indeed embraces the responsibilities of being an adult, a husband, and a father. He is a superb role model, teaching that manhood is often more about giving, caring, working, serving, and of course, loving than it is about selfishly following one's career ambitions.

Discussion Starters: *Explain how Mr. Holland understands the responsibilities of a being man. Discuss the irony that Mr. Holland is the father of a deaf child. Do you think that Mr. Holland's life was a success?*

PLACES IN THE HEART (1984)

This Depression-era story is about a woman (Sally Field playing Edna Spalding) who, suddenly widowed, decides to resist the community's efforts to force the sale of her farm. As good a portrait of the Dust Bowl period in the American Southwest as any ever filmed, it provides a primal lesson: that the places in one's heart, more than the geographical places, are the truly important places in life. The courage and love shown in this film are often startling in their intensity and move young people to tears.

Discussion Starters: *Why is it so important to Edna to "save the farm"? What role does the fear of not having enough money play in this story? What are some of the ways in which our society has changed, since the Great Depression, to protect people like the Spalding family?*

ROCKY (1976)

Rocky has become a cultural metaphor for inspirational underdog stories, but many boys, perhaps discovering the film for the first time, will be equally moved by its quiet moments of kindness and generosity: Rocky's making up with his old trainer following a quarrel; the mousy Adrian blossoming into a beautiful woman through Rocky's love for her; even the quiet, supportive friendship of his former boss, the loan shark. Through Rocky Balboa's eyes, boys learn what true manhood is made of, not just the ability to fight but the willingness and courage to grow and change.

Discussion Starters: *How is what happens to Rocky not just "dumb luck"? How does Rocky show that, in spite of his job as a low-class "enforcer" for a crook, he still has a good heart? Why do you think Rocky calls out for Adrian at the end of the movie?*

SEARCHING FOR BOBBY FISCHER (1993)

Against the backdrop of intense chess training and tournaments, *Searching for Bobby Fischer* explores the morality of children and competition with a sensitivity and intelligence. It is neither preachy nor black and white; nor is it filled with obvious and simple solutions. This film shows us the dangers of trying to make children live out the dreams of their parents. It is an indispensable story for boys with special gifts and for the parents, coaches, teachers, and mentors who must help them.

Discussion Starters: *Was something you liked to do ever "ruined" by too much pressure on you to keep doing it? How much should parents decide what activities are best for their kids? If you could be really great at one thing, what would it be?*

SILVERADO (1985)

The hero in any Western is decisive, brave, tough, and invariably knows right from wrong. Such a man is not complete by current standards, and yet he carries essential lessons. *Silverado* is a well-crafted Western about brave men cleaning up a corrupt town. These men assume honesty, expect difficulty and bad luck, and do not complain about it. The strong protect the weak. *Silverado* inspires boys toward bravery, doing the right thing, and trusting your friends and yourself.

Discussion Starters: *In the Old West a man sometimes had to kill another to fully be a man—what do you think of this? How can you achieve manhood differently today? How do Westerns like this one show us what kinds of relationships and challenges real men have? Do you trust yourself to do the right thing in every situation?*

STAND BY ME (1986)

This film is a classic about how boys nurture one another and yearn to be morally and emotionally cared for. Four boys are challenged to understand what is right and to try

to do it together. While suitable for boys ten and older, it does contain very coarse language. Younger audiences should definitely watch it in the presence of an adult who can help immediately with discussion. Its problematic qualities notwithstanding, this film is very fine and inspires parents, mentors, teachers, and students to explore such themes as right and wrong, loyalty to friends, parent-son relationships, and peer pressure.

Discussion Starters: *How do Gordie's friends, especially Chris, try to heal him? What does the writer mean when he says that you never have as a good friend again as the friends you have when you're twelve years old?*

VISION QUEST (1985)

A vision quest is a traditional Native American ritual in which a young man goes out, away from the safety of his family and tribe, to find "his place" in the world; he leaves a boy but returns a man. In this film Louden Swain, a high school wrestler, is seeking a championship but is also "wrestling" with more than just his opponents on the mat. Like young Native Americans, he learns what kind of man he is becoming. Louden is a good model for boys, as he becomes capable of overcoming great challenges. He also discovers in himself strength of character, self-sacrifice, discipline, commitment, and faith that he had not known he possessed.

Discussion Starters: *How is Louden prepared for his chal-*

lenges by what happened during his parents' divorce? What role does Louden's grandfather play in his life? Explain how doing something truly "hard" has rewards all its own.

WHITE SQUALL (1996)

Troubled young men, mentored by a husband and wife, face adversity within themselves, in nature, and in society when their ship is destroyed. This is a film not only about physical survival against an unforgiving ocean, but also about the aftermath: Who will take moral responsibility for the disaster? In viewing this film, each young man is challenged to face the moral confusion in his own life.

Discussion Starters: *What does this film say about the reality of "nature" and its unpredictability? Even though the captain acted responsibly, was there anything he could have done any differently to prevent the tragedy? If so, what does this say about the limits of responsibility?*

High School

ACCIDENTAL TOURIST, THE (1988)

Few stories have ever presented a better picture of how losing a child can affect the lives of the adults in that child's world. A strong picture of values and character unfolds as the protagonist, a travel writer whose son has been violently killed, learns to become more empathic and honest.

Discussion Starters: *Explain how Macon's attempt to control things all the time causes him to miss a lot of wonderful chances for fun. How does Muriel teach him that fun isn't something to fear? Talk about how this movie shows the pain caused by the death of a beloved son.*

THE ACCUSED (1988)

Appropriate only for mature boys, this study in group behavior is a rough, painful exploration of how men without a firm moral grounding can slip quickly and terrifyingly into animalistic acts. Prior to the rape of Jodie Foster's character, none of the men involved were criminals, yet they commit a terrible act. This film starkly teaches our sons that the pressure of mobs, peers, and groups can overwhelm a young man's good judgment and sense of decency. It also shows how he must redeem himself: by being honest, even if it means turning on his friends.

Discussion Starters: *Did you ever do something you didn't really want to do, just so other guys wouldn't think you were "chicken"? What language would you use to refuse to do something wrong, even though your friends were all doing it? What do you do in your everyday life to control urges and impulses that you know are wrong?*

BLOOD IN, BLOOD OUT
(also titled *Bound by Honor*) (1993)

A long but intensely powerful film about Latino inner-city males who struggle to find a moral center, this action- and drama-packed morality play follows the lives of three young men as they make intertwined moral choices. Each is challenged by crime, drugs, and gang pressures, and each strives to do what is right against the odds. Because of its violence

and language, it is not suitable for middle school or younger audiences. It is especially powerful for inner-city kids.

Discussion Starters: *Why is a gang a poor substitute for a real family? What does the violence in this movie say about the need for respect and responsibility among young men? Which of these young men do you most identify with, and why?*

BOYZ N THE HOOD (1991)

This hard-edged film about gangs and growing up black and male in the inner city is crucial viewing for high school boys. It depicts how an environment can strip males of one kind of honor and entice them with another. It avoids moral shortcuts and inspires in-depth dialogue about what young men need in order to feel whole.

Discussion Starters: *How does this film show that violence only leads to more violence? Why did Gandhi once say, "An eye for an eye, and someday, the whole world is blind"? Have you ever felt pressures from peers that frightened you?*

BRAVEHEART (1995)

Mel Gibson both starred in and directed this Academy Award–winning film about the Scottish patriot and martyr William Wallace. Although the scenes of sixteenth-century warfare are gruesome and bloody, they are necessary to portray how truly horrible war is. Wallace, nicknamed Braveheart for his courage and cunning on the battlefield, is an educated, thoughtful, and very moral "barbarian." His willingness to sacrifice in order to free Scotland from the unfair and cruel totalitarianism is at the center of the film.

Discussion Starters: *Why do you think this story begins with William Wallace as a young boy? Through his courage, Wallace leads his countrymen to freedom; was the price he paid worth it? When, in your life, would freedom become worth dying for?*

A BRONX TALE (1993)

In this moving father-son drama, the young boy called C is divided between love for his devoted, bus-driving father (played by Robert De Niro) and the lure of the street-smart, money-spending local gangster, Sonny (played by Chazz Palminteri). C's father and Sonny are two dramatically different types of mentors, and after Sonny takes the boy under his wing, C is forced to choose between them in the journey toward finding himself. C's father's monologue on the values of hard work and common decency is not to be missed.

Discussion Starters: *Who is the better mentor, C's father or Sonny? Is Sonny right that the working man is a "stiff"? How does C prove himself better than his street friends?*

CASABLANCA (1942)

Humphrey Bogart's Rick, a self-described "saloon-keeper," is the classic example of the American male of the World

War II era: tough, self-contained, independent, and possessing a strong moral code that includes honesty, empathy, self-sacrifice, and honor. When the woman who was the love of his life suddenly appears on his doorstep with her world-famous husband, a French Resistance hero, Rick faces serious moral questions. The complexity of the plot is partly determined by its historical context—the important but often-overlooked period just before America entered World War II and before the world became aware of the concentration camps and the Holocaust. Young men viewing Rick's dilemmas will be inspired to face their fears and moral challenges.

Discussion Starters: *What does Captain Renault mean when he says that Rick is "just like other men, only more so"? Explain why Rick is so hurt, and why he later realizes that his hurt is not the most important thing. How is Rick, in some ways, more admirable than the hero Victor Laszlo?*

CONTACT (1997)

When contact is finally made between Earth and extraterrestrials, many people respond fearfully, allowing their narrow view of religion to blind them to the possibility of God's role in the larger meaning of the events. This visually exciting film inspires a crucial dialogue about science and superstition, religious belief and reason. The unfolding action inspires boys toward the highest self-regard, and it ends in a vision of contact between the human being and the hidden soul that will need good, clear discussion with adults.

Discussion Starters: *How are science and religion actually saying similar things in this film? What did you admire most about the way Jodie Foster's character handled all the obstacles in her path? How does your spiritual vision affect your everyday life?*

THE DEER HUNTER (1978)

A group of friends in an industrial town in Pennsylvania try to do their patriotic best by enlisting in the army during the Vietnam War. Captured and tortured, the three friends miraculously escape and are changed forever by their experiences. In the end, what saves them is their core belief in the basic values of community, empathy, and personal honor, as well as the love and safety they find in one another. This deep and tormenting movie is to be viewed only by mature boys. Because of its thematic maturity, its violence, and the complex questions it poses, adults should be part of the viewing experience.

Discussion Starters: *Does the company of good and trusted friends make going off to war easier to accept? How does De Niro's "one shot" philosophy of life save him? When he goes back to try and save his friend, does he do the right thing in playing Russian roulette? Can you understand why he does this?*

THE EDGE (1997)

The title of this film is very fitting: Does a man really know how he might hold up on "the edge" of his abilities to think clearly, withstand pain and hunger, and make the best of a difficult situation? In this powerful psychological thriller about three men lost in the Alaskan wilderness, a man's values and moral strengths pull him through, coupled with the intelligence, calm perseverance, and quiet courage that are anyone's best allies in times of crisis.

Discussion Starters: *What does "dying of shame" mean, as it's mentioned in this film? What does "What one man can do, another man can do" mean? How much courage do you think you would need to stay calm and avoid shame on your "edge"?*

GALLIPOLI (1981)

This film painstakingly depicts the blossoming friendship between two young men on the eve of World War I, and then shows how one of the most ill-fated military campaigns of the twentieth century destroys them. *Gallipoli* provides an excellent opportunity to discuss the ambiguity of war and the sometime failure of command. Because of the film's violence and subject matter, only mature young men should see it.

Discussion Starters: *Did the men who died on this battlefield die for nothing? Would it, in a way, have taken more courage* *to refuse to advance than to go? How do the young men in the film make sacrifices for each other?*

GOOD WILL HUNTING (1997)

Will Hunting (played by Matt Damon) is a tough young man from Southie, a rough and rugged section of Boston, who has been in constant trouble with the law since he was a child. While working as a custodian at a university, he solves an incredibly complex math problem that was put up on a bulletin board for the most advanced mathematics students to ponder. Soon we see that Will is a genius not just in math but in any subject to which he gives his attention. The problem: how to get Will to stop his immoral, overly aggressive behavior. Two mentors and his boyhood friends try to help guide him to mature manhood, but in the end Will learns that he himself must make the decision to be a loving, wise, and reasonable man.

Discussion Starters: *Why do you think Will finally lets down his guard and talks to the counselor? What's more important to you: to be rich, to be smart, or to be happy? What does Will's psychologist mean at the end when he tells him, "It wasn't your fault"?*

HAMLET (1990)

This timeless story of a young prince avenging the death of his beloved father is compelling viewing, especially as it is performed by Mel Gibson in Franco Zeffirelli's 1990 version. This film is sit-thruable and Gibson plays Hamlet with an intensity that makes the character come to life. "To thine own self be true," "Neither a borrower nor a lender be," "To be or not to be, that is the question"—these are just some of the lines that inspire moral dialogue with young men, as does the tragedy of Hamlet himself: that a dutiful son, in these circumstances, still may end up sacrificing himself.

Discussion Starters: *What does this story say about conscience and its role in guilt and anxiety? How does* Hamlet *show the moral competencies of self-sacrifice, honor, and responsibility? Would you act differently from the way Hamlet did?*

IN AND OUT (1997)

Howard Brackett (played by Kevin Kline) is a dapper, beloved teacher at an affluent rural high school. Admired by his students and poised for marriage, Mr. Brackett seems to have it all. Yet his world is turned topsy-turvy when a former student unknowingly "outs" him as a gay man on national television, and Brackett has to discover who his friends really are—and who he is. This funny, touching movie is ultimately deeply affirming of the core American values of inclusion, self-respect, and respect for one's neighbor. Suitable for all boys, it may be especially useful to gay youths and their families.

Discussion Starters: *What qualities make Mr. Brackett such a good teacher? Why do some of his colleagues remove him from* *his job, and what are their motives? If you were Mr. Brackett's student, what would you do? Why?*

INSIDE MOVES (1980)

Inside moves are the ways a basketball player handles himself "inside," under the basket, where things get crowded and rough. (In "100 Books," see *The Moves Make the Man,* page 114). Each of us, as young men, must learn our own "inside moves." Roary, the protagonist, learns, almost too late, that suicide is not the answer to his problems, and that honesty, fairness, and loyalty are what really count in life.

Discussion Starters: *What important things in your life "move" inside your heart and spirit? What does this film suggest are the more important "inside moves" that occur in the growth of a man's soul? How does Roary learn that he is "big" and has value as a person?*

JUDGMENT AT NUREMBERG (1961)

The atrocities committed during World War II by Hitler and his supporters, especially the Holocaust, cried out for justice in 1945. *Judgment at Nuremberg,* a taut courtroom drama, is a careful and deeply dramatic presentation of the ways in which the world's need—and each person's individual need—for justice was satisfied. This film provides boys a very important story about fairness, honor, and decency.

Discussion Starters: *What do you know about World War II and about concentration camps? What do you think of the excuse that someone was "just following orders" in doing something obviously wrong? What words would you use to refuse to follow an order that is against your conscience?*

KRAMER VS. KRAMER (1979)

The French toast scene alone makes this movie a treasure of father-son pain and dynamics. The battle of *both* parents to hold on to their son through the horrors of divorce makes this a profoundly moving work of cinematic art. A groundbreaking story for its time, dealing so honestly with a boy's heartbreak, loss, and inner strength, *Kramer vs. Kramer* reveals that, amid the pain of divorce, we can learn tremendous lessons about ourselves and about our love for each other.

Discussion Starters: *Have there been any divorces in your family or circle of friends? How does this story help you to better understand them? How does the dad, by being forced to care for his son alone, become a better man? In the end, do you feel that the best thing happens?*

LIFE IS BEAUTIFUL (1998)

Hiding his little son while he works as a slave laborer in a Nazi concentration camp, a father (played by Italian filmmaker Roberto Benigni) manages to convince the boy that, as difficult as their life is, it is really just an exciting game, more about challenge and triumph than about despair. Relying on his courage, love, and deep sense of responsibility, the father overcomes the ultimate attack on the human spirit, and protects his son's reality amid the most horrible of circumstances.

Discussion Starters: *Why does the father have to lie to his son? Is the lie justified in this situation? Explain how attitude often matters more than events.*

A MAN FOR ALL SEASONS (1966)

This is the story of Thomas More, for whom the imperatives and demands of conscience guide him at all times and in all ways, regardless of personal consequences. Serving under Henry VIII, More (played brilliantly by Paul Scofield) must resist his king's edicts in order to stand by his own love of God. Although the historical setting might confuse some younger viewers, explaining it is a great way to talk about this story's theme: that while there are huge consequences to standing up for what you believe, the costs of not doing so are even higher.

Discussion Starters: *What is a man for all seasons? Why does Thomas More refuse to grant the king what he wants? What does this story teach about faith and conscience?*

THE MATRIX (1999)

Plato's "allegory of the cave" meets a Christ-like figure of salvation in this science fiction thriller. Although there is a fifteen-minute period of extreme and gratuitously stylized violence toward the end of this film, the intelligence of the plot and the complexity of the themes make it very worthwhile nonetheless for stimulating moral and spiritual dialogue. Much can be learned by young men about the need to trust themselves, wonder over their destiny, do the right thing, and try to understand what is real as they move through life.

Discussion Starters: *Was Neo truly the "chosen one"? Was there a time in your life when something that seemed to be happening actually wasn't, and you had to second-guess yourself? How would you define "real power"?*

MISSISSIPPI BURNING (1988)

Mississippi Burning tells the powerful story of how two FBI agents, who differ from each other in almost every way, find common ground to solve the disappearance of three young civil rights workers in a small Mississippi town. This story teaches boys how to work together for fairness, and how teamwork helps us overcome difficulties that would be impossible to overcome alone.

Discussion Starters: *Why is Anderson (the agent played by Gene Hackman) able to rise above his own background to do his duty? Does this movie convince you that "bending" the rules to* *right a wrong is sometimes justifiable? How is violence used to control people in this story, and why does it fail in the end?*

OCTOBER SKY (1999)

This is a moving, true story about a boy who has to juggle his desire to be a rocket scientist with his moral duty to his family and town. This film asks: How can a young man be free to find himself while still doing what's right by those he loves? Every high-school-age male must face this question in his own way if he is to fully become a man.

Discussion Starters: *How does Homer prove to everyone that he deserves a chance to follow his dream? How does his teacher help Homer find the courage to go for it? How does Homer resolve the conflict between his need to be himself and his need to do his duty to his family?*

PATHS OF GLORY (1957)

For any boy who thinks war is "cool," this classic depicts the brutal realities and moral agonies of World War I. A harsh film that should be seen only by mature boys, *Paths of Glory* can stimulate powerful moral dialogue about just and unjust forms of authority.

Discussion Starters: *In what ways does this movie show that "war is hell"? In what other ways, besides going to war, can a man show his bravery? Should a man ever disobey orders?*

THE PRINCE OF TIDES (1991)

A violent rape of a mother and daughter has been hidden and covered up by the family, which years later haunts everyone involved. Because these events are not shown until the end of the film, young men watching the struggles of the now-grown son (Nick Nolte) and his siblings, as well as the intervention of a psychiatrist (Barbra Streisand), will have to struggle with the moral and psychological difficulties right along with the family. In the end, young men will realize that not dealing with a trauma, however painful, has a terribly high price: one way or another, it will affect us later, and either we take control of it, or the memories will control us.

Discussion Starters: *How does this story show the differences between good and bad secrets? When Nolte threatens to drop the violin, is he justified? How is the ending of this story happy and sad at the same time?*

SAVING PRIVATE RYAN (1998)

This World War II film is very much about the male search for self-worth. Captain Miller and a few men strike out across France to try to find Private Ryan, whose three brothers have already been killed. They each learn about duty and the terrible toll of war. As Ryan remembers the incident from his own old age, he wonders if he has earned the right to remain alive. The violence in this film makes it unsuitable for boys younger than middle adolescence.

Discussion Starters: *How is this a story about living a worthy and good life? Why is war ever necessary—does this film help answer that question? Are you living a worthwhile life?*

SCENT OF A WOMAN (1992)

This film is a brilliant portrait of the complex dynamics of a mentoring relationship. Al Pacino plays an angry ex-colonel who wants to kill himself, and Chris O'Donnell is a young prep school student who won't let him. In the end, courage, friendship, loyalty, and love between men are portrayed with passion and depth. A man in despair finds hope by becoming the moral voice of a confused community, and a boy becomes a man by acting according to his conscience, without faltering. This film is filled with foul language, so be forewarned.

Discussion Starters: *In what ways is Frank brave, and in what ways is he cowardly? How do some of the rich boys at the school show a lack of responsibility and moral fiber?* (See Dead Poets Society, *page 47, for an interesting comparison.) What do you think of Frank's speech toward the end about courage and honor?*

SCHINDLER'S LIST (1993)

This now-classic depiction of the Holocaust provides a forum for discussing the character both of nations and of individuals. The industrialist Schindler starts out exploiting a group of Jews for profit against the backdrop of the Holocaust but ends up saving as many as he can. This movie is brutally honest about human violence and should be seen only by mature young men.

Discussion Starters: *Is there evil in the world, in your view? What is evil? What did Schindler do that was extraordinary? Have you ever given in to peer pressure, as the Germans did to the Nazis, and regretted the results?*

THE SHAWSHANK REDEMPTION (1994)

The Shawshank Redemption is the story of Andy (played by Tim Robbins), who is imprisoned for a murder he did not commit at Shawshank Prison, a primitive and dangerously corrupt institution. He suffers terribly in his early days at Shawshank, but with the help of a friend (played by Morgan Freeman) he finds solace, courage, and meaning. Redemption, we learn from his story, can exist in *any* environment and is needed in anyone's life, even the innocent's. A few intense scenes might make this film difficult for some younger high school viewers.

Discussion Starters: *Even though he didn't kill his wife, why does Andy feel that he is still "responsible" for her death? Look up the word* redemption, *and think of different ways, different situations where you could use it. Why does Red admire Andy so much, and how are both of these men teachers to each other?*

A SIMPLE PLAN (1998)

This movie presents a moral allegory about men who bring about their own demise with one simple immoral act, the theft of money from a crashed plane. It is a superb starting point for discussions about the nature of morality, how we become tempted away from moral competency, how one bad act can snowball into tragedy, and how our personal ethics can become muddied once we start trying to rationalize bad behavior. The movie's violence and its themes make it appropriate only for mature boys.

Discussion Starters: *What would you do if you "found" a huge sum of money? How does the money ruin the lives of the characters in this story?*

UNFORGIVEN (1992)

This Clint Eastwood film is said to have changed the Western genre forever. While somewhat of an exaggeration, the claim makes sense from a moral standpoint. A wife he nearly worships for her moral strength transforms William Munny, a former thief and killer, into a good man, but once she's gone, he is challenged to be moral on his own. Suitable only for high-school-age boys, this film challenges viewers to decide what part inborn character, alcohol addiction, environment, friendships, and love all play in the development of ethics and morality.

Discussion Starters: *How is the title of this film, in some ways, ironic? What does Munny feel when he gets so sick after being beaten up? Is every man capable of terrible behavior? Is every man capable of being redeemed?*

100

100

BOOKS

Preschool/ Kindergarten

AESOP'S FABLES

These easy-to-read little stories with big morals, published in various fine editions, might be read aloud to any growing boy, even before he can have a dialogue about them. Aesop wrote mainly about human character but used animal figures, making the tales perfect for the toddler or early-school-age child. To be sure the messages of these fables get through, especially to the younger boy, it's important to ask questions in his language about their lessons regarding honesty, fairness, self-sacrifice, and duty. The end of each fable provides numerous discussion starters.

THE BOY WHO HELD BACK THE SEA by Thomas Locker, illustrated by Lenny Holt

One day on his way home from skipping church, Jan, who is always getting in trouble, sees a terrifying sight: a leak in the dike that protects the town from the sea. Jan quickly puts his finger over the leak and saves the town. While watching Jan do the right thing and stick with it, every boy, even the most rambunctious, sees how to focus his energy to the good.

Discussion Starters: *Should the grown-ups who ignored Jan be sorry for what they did? Do you agree that even if you make mistakes you can still be a good person?*

THE BUTTER BATTLE BOOK by Dr. Seuss

The people on one side of the Wall butter their bread "butter side up." The people on the other side butter theirs "butter side down." From this seemingly trivial difference grows a sad and poignant war between the Zooks and the Yooks. Dr. Seuss's classic, like so many of his books, teaches large moral lessons through small imaginative parables and excitingly drawn characters. Written during the cold war, this book is not just for kids but for adults who might forget that if we're going to fight, we'd better have a very good reason, or the human soul can be lost.

Discussion Starters: *Why are the Zooks and the Yooks so*

mad at each other? Do they have a good reason? Do you have good reasons for the fights you get into?

DRUMMER BOY by Ann Warren Turner,
illustrated by Mark Hess

"Who would've ever thought I'd go to war—a boy like me?" Thus begins this sad, moving story of a thirteen-year-old farm boy who joins the Union Army after Abraham Lincoln visits his small town. This picture book covers a remarkable range of emotions, from excitement to fear to grief to a quiet, reserved worldliness. War is a terrible thing, and through the eyes of a child, it is even more terrible, yet the drummer boy learns valuable lessons about loyalty, self-sacrifice, honor, and responsibility.

    Discussion Starters: *Why do you think the boy went into the war? Was the boy a coward for hiding at his first battle? What did the boy want to say to President Lincoln when the war was over?*

THE EMPEROR'S NEW CLOTHES
by Hans Christian Andersen,
illustrated by Virginia Lee Burton

This classic fairy tale made its way into the language, and its wonderful satirical portrait of people who were afraid to tell the emperor the truth became a metaphor in popular culture. It takes one brave, innocent boy to finally tell the truth. Because of him, all boys can learn that truth-telling takes great courage and risk.

Discussion Starters: *Can you think of a time when telling the truth was a scary thing to do? Should you tell the truth even if it hurts someone's feelings? Do you think that the boy who told the truth was heroic?*

THE GIVING TREE by Shel Silverstein

This book tells the heart-wrenching story of a tree that sacrifices everything for a little boy. Even upon becoming an adult, the boy does not seem to fully appreciate the tree's self-sacrifice. But readers understand and are inspired toward compassion. A reading of this story to a boy should be accompanied by good conversation about selfishness.

Discussion Starters: *Can you think of a time when you cared too much about yourself and not enough about someone else? Why is giving as important as getting?*

THE GROUCHY LADYBUG by Eric Carle

This classic picture book tells the story of a wonderful anti-hero: a not-very-nice ladybug who is always trying to pick a fight and never says please or thank you. Despite this little bug's bad manners, you can't help but admire his spunk. Yet in the end this combative little ladybug realizes that being himself, eating aphids, and saving leaves is

enough—he doesn't need to be obnoxious or a pretender to power.

Discussion Starters: *What does this story teach about being brave, regardless of how big or little we are? When you're grouchy, do you sometimes forget your best manners? Why did the ladybug become nicer in the end?*

ISLAND BABY by Holly Keller

An old man, Pops, saves injured birds, healing them and sending them back into nature. A little boy named Simon finds a baby flamingo, and Pops helps Simon to save this "island baby." This is a sweet, meaningful story about a mentoring relationship at its best (every boy would love to have a grandpa like Pops) and the importance of caring for animals and for the weak. Kindness, decency, and service are all-important lessons offered by this richly illustrated book.

Discussion Starters: *What did Simon learn from Pops that was even more important than how to save Baby? Do you think that people should be kind to animals and try to help them? Why?*

THE MAN WHO KEPT HIS HEART IN A BUCKET
by Sonia Levitin, illustrated by Jerry Pinkney

When Jack's heart is broken, he wants to be certain that he never has to feel that bad again. Because he is a metalworker, he knows how to build a metal box to carry his heart in, so that it is protected even though it's not much use to him. Wonderful drawings and the pretty maiden who saves Jack from himself make this story truly sing for young boys. Filled with lessons of empathy, honesty, and an odd kind of honor, it teaches that you need to risk having your heart hurt to get the great things in life.

Discussion Starters: *Explain how having a broken heart is a lot like having your feelings hurt. Have your feelings ever been hurt? Did Jack learn that it's okay to be sad sometimes?*

MY LITTLE BOOK ABOUT GOD by Jane Werner Watson, illustrated by Eloise Wilkin

This collection of stories gives children a sense of spiritual security. It is best read aloud to your son; as he gets older, he may enjoy reading it aloud to you. In this storybook, God gives each of us an inner voice that teaches right from wrong. As you read this book to him, your little boy will benefit from questions you pose about the voice of God that is inside him.

Discussion Starters: *Whisper to yourself, "It's good to be kind." Now whisper it just inside your mind, without saying the words out loud at all—are those words God talking? Do this with all the words God tells in this story.*

THE PAPER CRANE by Molly Garrett Bang

When their restaurant is left without customers (somebody moved the highway!), a father and son struggle to make ends meet. Then a stranger arrives; to reward their kindness to him, he uses his ability to make origami cranes, which come to life, to save the business. This magical little story teaches that kindness, especially if shown at times when it is most difficult to do so, can pay big dividends.

Discussion Starters: *Think of a time when somebody was nice to you, just because they wanted to be. What are some ways that you could be a kinder person?*

PLANE SONG by Diane Siebert, illustrated by Vincent Nasta

For little boys who love airplanes, *Plane Song* will be a favorite book. Surprisingly, it has an important moral to teach as well, in that it shows how flying requires personal responsibility. The book climaxes with a wonderful illustration and the words "planes for work and planes for fun / and in the cockpit of each one / there sits a pilot in command— / a pilot with a steady hand." This is a character trait to which all boys aspire.

Discussion Starters: *What does it mean to have a steady hand? Airplanes can be very dangerous unless the pilot is very careful—can you think of other dangerous things? Are you a careful pilot?*

THE SNOWY DAY by Ezra Jack Keats

Published in 1962 and still popular, *The Snowy Day* has rightfully become a modern classic. On the surface, it's a very simple story. Young Peter awakens to find out that it has snowed the night before, and we follow him through the excitement and fun of a "snowy day." Yet this book is also a wonderful opportunity to teach empathy to our very young sons, as it clicks in their minds how they have felt just like Peter, enjoying their own snowy days.

   Discussion Starters: *Have you ever been excited to wake up to a snowy day? Do you have as much fun when it snows as Peter did?*

STEVIE by John Steptoe

This touching, illustrated story of early friendship and loss between two African-American boys shows how boys can hide their affection for each other—even from themselves. It is just right to be read aloud to children up to school age or given to a boy who is beginning his first reading experience.

   Discussion Starters: *What does this story teach about the importance of honesty in friendships? Explain empathy and point out examples of it from this story.*

WHAT IS GOD? by Etan Boritzer,
illustrated by Robbie Marantz

For people who have left traditional religion but still seek
a universal spiritual life, this is a classic in rhyming prose. It
pays homage to all the world's religions, and to the sense in
each of them that there is a greater force caring for us all.

Discussion Starters: *When you pray, do you feel God listening? How can God be good if bad things sometimes happen in
life? Explain the phrase "Let go and let God."*

WHERE THE WILD THINGS ARE by Maurice Sendak

A marvelous tale of adventure and imagination, this story is
a perfect place to start teaching energetic little boys that just
because they are being disciplined or punished does not
mean they're not loved.

Discussion Starters: *Is it fair that Max should be punished
when he misbehaves? If you could travel far away and rule the wild
things, what would you miss most about home? What's the best
thing about being loved "the most of all"?*

WILLIAM AND THE GOOD OLD DAYS
by Eloise Greenfield, illustrated by
Jan Spivey Gilchrist

Although William is just a little boy, he longs for the "good
old days" when his grandma, now sick, was healthy and

they had fun together. *William and the Good Old Days* is a wonderful story for teaching little ones their first lessons about losing people we love (especially older family members like grandparents). This richly illustrated book ends with powerful messages about respect, honor, and love.

Discussion Starters: *Why is William angry that his grandma is so sick? If your grandma got sick, how would you feel? Discuss the seasons, especially winter and how everything that lives must die someday, too.*

YO! YES? by Chris Raschka

This is a story about an interracial friendship between two young boys, one who is quite shy and the other who is very outgoing and friendly. An important book to help our sons continue building their color-blindness when it comes to people, this Caldecott Honor Book also teaches empathy, respect, decency, and the importance of these things in building friendships.

Discussion Starters: *Do you know any shy boys? Any outgoing ones? Are you more shy or outgoing yourself? How did this book show (in the picture) the two boys becoming good friends at the end?*

Elementary School

Lower Grades 1–3

FIRESTORM AT KOOKABURRA STATION by Robert Elmer

Two teenage brothers, Patrick and Michael, are rescued from a firestorm and other perils by Ibrahim, a large man with a scarred face who is later falsely accused of being a criminal. The boys must decide whether and how to help him. An important story about honesty, loyalty, and responsibility, this book teaches boys to stand up for what they think is right—to listen to their hearts.

Discussion Starters: *Why do so many people incorrectly agree that Ibrahim is a criminal? How do you think we can best* *help people who have severe disabilities or scars? What enables Ibrahim to forgive his accusers and save their lives even at the risk of losing his own?*

THE COMPLETE GRIMM'S FAIRY TALES (Pantheon Edition)

These stories are a treasure of moral allegory, as are other fairy-tale collections from all over the world. Throughout human history, teachers and parents have used fairy tales to describe symbolic and allegorical journeys to moral life. All homes and classrooms will benefit from bringing fairy tales out of the nursery school and returning them to the fore-front of moral teaching. Once I even used a Grimm's fairy tale to facilitate a discussion among five hundred middle and high school students about teen pregnancy. All of us were mesmerized by how powerfully a tale many thousands of years old mirrored the issues faced by today's young people.

LIKE JAKE AND ME by Mavis Jukes, illustrated by Lloyd Bloom

In Alex's eyes, Jake, his stepfather, is the strongest, toughest guy alive. When, ironically, it turns out that Jake is terrified of spiders, Alex has a chance to "rescue" Jake from a spider, giving Alex a way to feel empowered and closer to his mentor.

Discussion Starters: *Do you have a stepfather, or do you know anybody who does? When Alex and Jake dance around the*

house together, how does that make Alex feel? Can you see that for some boys a stepfather is just as "real" a dad as any other dad?

THE LITTLE PRINCE by Antoine de Saint-Exupéry

This intergalactic fable takes the little prince to Earth, where a fox teaches him the secret of life. If you are reading it aloud to a child, you should go slowly and let the child (and you) savor it. It electrifies the imagination, and its lessons can become the heart of family discussions over a period of weeks.

Discussion Starters: *How is the little prince loyal, fair, and honest? What does this story teach about self-sacrifice?*

LOU GEHRIG: THE LUCKIEST MAN by David A. Adler, illustrated by Terry Widener

When he was forced to retire from baseball at the age of thirty-five, after having played fourteen seasons without missing a single game, Lou Gehrig, stricken with a terrible terminal illness, said that he was "the luckiest man alive." Because of the wonderful life he enjoyed, and Gehrig's legend of service, responsibility, and self-sacrifice, any boy does well to remember him. The movie *The Pride of the Yankees* covers the same territory (see "100 Movies," page 28), but this book is well worth the time, and the message merits retelling.

Discussion Starters: *Not only did Lou Gehrig never miss a* *ball game, he never missed a day of school, either—do you think more than coincidence is at work there? Talk about feeling lucky and about the balance between good luck and bad in your life.*

THE MINSTREL IN THE TOWER by Gloria Skurzynski, illustrated by Julek Heller

A boy and his younger sister, living in medieval France, are threatened with becoming orphans when their father fails to return from the Crusades and their mother falls ill. When their mother sends them off to find an uncle who might be able to help, their poignant adventure begins. Filled with lessons of loyalty, responsibility, honesty, and fairness, yet told with all the excitement of an adventure story, this little novel is a good lesson builder for boys in general—and perhaps, in particular, boys with little sisters who occasionally get on their nerves!

Discussion Starters: *How does Roger prove to Alice how much he cares about her? How do the brother and sister work together to escape their captors, and what does this part of the book teach about teamwork?*

MINT COOKIE MIRACLES by Nancy Simpson

Dan, a new kid on the block, bullies Alex, who eventually extends the hand of friendship to him. This opens Dan's heart to his pain, anger, and resentment at being abandoned by his father, feelings that he now learns to express more appropriately. Teaching valuable lessons in empathy and compassion, this story inspires boys to see beyond behavior into intentions and causes, an important step in elementary-age moral development.

Discussion Starters: *Are the bullies you know just mean people, our could other things be making them angry? What happens to us on the inside when we refuse to forgive those who have hurt us? In what ways can you try to be a friend to a bully?*

THE STORIES JULIAN TELLS by Ann Cameron, illustrated by Ann Strugnell

Two brothers, Julian and Huey, have a variety of quiet, amusing, very realistic "adventures." Loved and nurtured by both their parents and taught right from wrong by a kind and deeply caring father, their lives are filled with warmth, humor, and friendship. Decency, empathy, and honesty are evident in these simple joyous stories, proving that not all moral character has to come out of suffering. Good values are part of these brothers' everyday lives, and the boys are excellent role models.

Discussion Starters: *What kind of a "whipping" and "beating" do Julian and Huey get for eating all the lemon cake their dad had made for their mom? What do you learn from listening to Julian talk about working in their little garden?*

STUART LITTLE by E. B. White, illustrated by
Garth Williams

Stuart Little is a human boy who looks exactly like a mouse.
Any boy can see what fun it would be to soar around the
lake in Central Park in a tiny mouse-sized speedboat, or to
tool around Manhattan in a nifty little sports car. Yet more
importantly, Stuart's friendship with the bird Margalo
demonstrates his loyalty, self-sacrifice, and empathy as strong
moral attributes. Boys will learn that friendship requires devotion and dedication.

    Discussion Starters: *Why does Stuart go out to find Mar-
galo? What does Stuart tell the children is most important, when
he has a chance to be their teacher? If you ever had a chance to be
an animal on the outside but still a human on the inside, what animal would you be?*

WHEN DINOSAURS DIE by Laurie Krasny Brown
and Marc Tolon Brown

Through the lives of a modern dinosaur family—they look
almost human and could live next door to you—young
readers learn what death is and how to handle it compas-
sionately. Deep feelings are explored as Harriet the hamster
dies and is given a memorial service. This book will open
feelings in school-age boys who may not have been able to
explore issues of death and loss directly before.

Discussion Starters: *What do you think happens when a person dies? What do the dinosaurs think?*

THE WIND IN THE WILLOWS by Kenneth Grahame, illustrated by Ernest H. Shepard

Isn't there always a Toad in every group of guys, a kid who, regardless of the good counsel of his pals, just can't stop himself from seeking the next adventure? At the very heart of *The Wind in the Willows* is the story of how Toad's friends keep saving his hide. This classic tale has much to teach our boys about the loyalty and responsibility required of true friendship.

Discussion Starters: *Why does Toad always get into trouble? What does it say about Toad's friends that they are always there for him? How do the heroes win back Toad Hall from the mean and creepy weasels?*

WINGMAN by Daniel Pinkwater

A mean teacher causes Donald Chen, the only Chinese-American student at his school, to stop attending school altogether. Donald loves comic books and spends his days daydreaming of comic book adventures, until he meets a wonderful superhero named Wingman. Brought back to school by a truant officer, Donald gets a new teacher, one who recognizes and even encourages Donald's love of comics. This story teaches empathy, honesty, and the enormous importance of kindness.

Discussion Starters: *Have you ever felt like an outsider, or that you just didn't fit in? How does Donald use his special talents to overcome these feelings? Why is it so important for Donald to meet the right kind of adult, one who really does care about him?*

Upper Grades 4–6

BLACK BEAUTY by Anna Sewell

This classic Victorian story follows a horse from its carefree days as a colt to its later terrible abuse at the hands of cruel owners. As they bond with Black Beauty, boys learn valuable lessons in friendship, fairness, and loyalty. Equally valuable is the clear picture they develop of bullies and the understanding that the decent and honorable thing for any boy or man to do is to protect the innocent and defenseless from cruelty.

Discussion Starters: *Why are the second owners of Black Beauty so mean in their treatment of the horse? What does this story teach you about responsibility?*

BRIDGE TO TERABITHIA by Katherine Paterson, illustrated by Donna Diamond

While it is extremely sad, this story of Jess, Leslie, and their imaginary land of Terabithia is written with great compassion. When Leslie drowns, we see Jess going through all the stages of grieving. Even if a boy reads it but doesn't want to talk about it, this novel gives him the opportunity to think about his own mortality and explore friendship, loss, loyalty, and personal responsibility.

Discussion Starters: *Is Jess responsible for Leslie's death? Was Leslie irresponsible? Did she disregard her own personal safety? Have you ever done something dangerous without thinking about the dangers? Have you ever thought about the "what ifs" of a situation?*

CHARLOTTE'S WEB by E. B. White

This wonderful book about the friendship between a pig named Wilbur and a spider named Charlotte has so many dimensions of beauty and values that one hardly knows where to start. Perhaps the most important is the way in which Charlotte, so loyal, honest, empathic, and kind, sacrifices all, in the end, to save a friend. The beautifully crafted relationships between the animal and human characters and between the animals themselves add even greater strength to the message.

Discussion Starters: *How is Wilbur's first reaction to Char-*

lotte wrong? Why do you think Charlotte helps Wilbur so much? What is the saddest part of this story, and why do you think it happened?

THE CHRONICLES OF NARNIA by C. S. Lewis

Heroes, heroines, giants, magic, God, wizards, witches, swords, battles, banquets, love, loss—all these themes and more are covered in these seven volumes by one of this century's foremost authorities on Christianity. The *Chronicles* are fantastical, filled with spiritual and moral allegory. In reading or talking about them with your son, you might call special attention to the moral decision making that each of the children goes through, and the way these decisions are often inspired by the divine figure, the lion Aslan. While elementary school is the perfect time for a child to begin discovering Narnia, a fairly mature reading level is helpful.

Discussion Starters: *What do these stories teach you about respect? Why is Aslan a character deserving great honor?*

THE CURSE OF THE BLUE FIGURINE by John Bellairs

A boy, Johnny Dixon, is given a magical ring that helps him defeat bullies but also exposes his own dark side. *The Curse of the Blue Figurine* is filled with important moral lessons about honor, self-respect, and loyalty; a mild horror story, it is told in a genre some boys like, with powerful moral messages.

Discussion Starters: *Explain how Johnny's early feelings of powerlessness set him up to be manipulated by Mr. Beard. Although he is a little bit crazy, what is the best character trait of Professor Coote? What does this story teach about unchecked power? In some ways, isn't the magical ring kind of like a weapon?*

DEFEAT OF THE GHOST RIDERS by Dave and Neta Jackson, illustrated by Julian Jackson

This beautifully illustrated adventure story focuses on the struggles of black families to survive in a world where only whites were allowed to prosper. It teaches important lessons in fairness, decency, responsibility, and empathy. The story is gripping, and boys learn that it is only right and fair to treat everyone with respect, whether black or white, rich or poor.

Discussion Starters: *What does Mary mean when she claims that "a soft answer turns away wrath"? Is it true? What experiences have you had with angry people, and how did you respond? In what ways do these black people pay for their freedom?*

A GATHERING OF DAYS by Joan W. Blos

This novel, written as a thirteen-year-old girl's journal and set in the early 1800s, examines slavery and oppression. It presents a very personal view of the plight of the early American settlers, and it is a powerful encouragement to boys in their development of empathy, decency, and fairness. Some boys, after reading it, have begun journals of their own life experiences.

Discussion Starters: *How does Catherine compare the death of her mother to the death of Cassy? Is either death more painful to her? What kind of emotions does Teacher Holt stir up when he reads the "slavery" articles to the students? What forms of oppression do you see in today's world? How does writing in the journal help Catherine? Do you think that writing in a journal could be helpful to you?*

THE INDIAN IN THE CUPBOARD by Lynne Reid Banks

A fantasy story filled with practical, commonsense ethics, *The Indian in the Cupboard* is the story of Omri, who is given a gift of a small cabinet and a toy Indian figurine. The challenge to figure out right from wrong starts in earnest when Omri learns that in spite of the small dimensions of his new friend, there are huge responsibilities that come with having power over the lives of others, and the challenge to figure out right from wrong begins in earnest.

Discussion Starters: *If you were God, how would you change the world to make it better? What does Omri figure out, that his friend Patrick doesn't, about being "in charge" of other human beings? Think about the word* gift *and what it really means.*

ISLAND OF THE BLUE DOLPHINS by Scott O'Dell

Karana is a twelve-year-old Native American girl stranded and all alone on an island. Her fellow tribesmen have left, and her little brother has been killed. But this tale covers more than her survival issues; she also demonstrates self-esteem, forgiveness, empathy, and a host of other moral competencies. Finally, Karana befriends both a wild dog and another little girl, the child of a mortal enemy tribe.

Discussion Starters: *How in your life have you had to be like Karana, even if you weren't stranded alone on an island? Why does Karana develop a deeper calmness as this story goes on?*

THE PHANTOM TOLLBOOTH by Norton Juster, illustrated by Jules Feiffer

Getting into a special magical car, Milo drives through a tollbooth and finds himself in a whole different world. In sharing this story with boys, we teach them that they possess a phantom tollbooth of their own that requires only a little courage and imagination to drive through. But who does a boy become in his world of imagination? What qualities of character and values does he exhibit? Each boy must answer this, and we must help him.

Discussion Starters: *Why is Milo an especially good candidate to receive a phantom tollbooth? What does Milo learn about himself in his new world? What does the expression "jumping to conclusions" mean?*

SEES BEHIND TREES by Michael Dorris

Walnut lives with his tribe, a century or two before the arrival of the white man. By learning to listen deeply, he comes to accept who he is and how to compensate for his weaknesses. By reading about his experiences, boys learn that everyone has special gifts—moral, spiritual, and practical—to bring to the community in which they live.

Discussion Starters: *Can you think of other famous people who overcame their "disabilities" and became great? How does Grey Fire's faith help Sees Behind Trees to believe in himself? Think about "seeing" (as in the expression "I see what you mean")—can you sometimes "see" what can't be seen, too?*

STUCK IN NEUTRAL by Terry Trueman

This short novel is told from the point of view of a fourteen-year-old boy named Shawn McDaniel who is profoundly disabled: He can neither talk nor respond to cues from his caregivers. But he has a spiritual and moral point of view that is startlingly powerful. The novel raises questions not only about what might be going on inside the minds of those we consider retarded (in the way *Flowers for Algernon* did a generation ago) but also about a family's and culture's duty to the severely disabled.

Discussion Starters: *How can a father ever contemplate killing his own child out of love? What does this story teach about attitudes toward "handicapped" people?*

THE WHIPPING BOY by Sid Fleischman,
illustrated by Peter Sis

Imagine having someone to take all your punishments—
your "whippings"—for you when you do wrong. *The
Whipping Boy* is the story of a spoiled young prince whose
whipping boy saves him pain but also teaches him the
meaning of true friendship.

Discussion Starters: *What would be the problem with somebody else taking your punishments for you? How did the whipping
boy prove himself to be loyal and responsible, and what did the
prince learn from this self-sacrifice?*

Middle
School

ANIMAL FARM by George Orwell

"All pigs are equal . . . but some pigs are more equal than others." George Orwell, in his two greatest works, *1984* and *Animal Farm,* demonstrated his amazing understanding of the nuances of language, and how the subtle twisting of words and phrases can control thinking and behavior. Given the immense power of the media in our children's lives, his gifts as a writer are still remarkably useful. While *Animal Farm* is, on the surface, a story about the struggle for power in a barnyard world, it is actually a powerful lesson in holding on to one's moral center and sense of responsibility while the world is going crazy.

Discussion Starters: *What is Orwell suggesting when he* *says that some pigs are "more equal" than others? What are some of the ways, other than brute force, that a person can control and gain power? What is the main difference between promising that everyone will get an equal chance and promising that everyone will be equal?*

BLESS THE BEASTS AND CHILDREN
by Glendon Swarthout

Perfect for middle school readers as well as adults, this short novel tells the vivid story of a band of adolescent outcasts at a summer camp for boys. Although ultimately tragic, the book can generate a powerful discussion about anger between kids and parents, and the ways kids sometimes torment one another.

Discussion Starters: *What could the boys have done differently to avoid the tragic ending yet still maintain their honor? What is the author saying about how some children are raised today? How are the boys similar to the buffalo they try to save?*

THE CALL OF THE WILD by Jack London

Buck, a dog, is stolen from his home and thrust into the merciless life of the Arctic north during the Klondike gold rush, where he is forced to endure hardship, bitter cold, and the savage lawlessness of man and beast. He becomes a role model to humans, including any boy who reads his story. Because London's use of language provides a stunning example of visual writing, his graphic descriptions of animal abuse may be difficult for some younger readers. In all, however, this story teaches valuable lessons in loyalty, honor, service, and fairness.

Discussion Starters: *Is Buck a hero? At what point do goals become a negative thing? Have you ever set a goal that turned out to be negative rather that positive?*

DR. JEKYLL AND MR. HYDE by Robert Louis Stevenson

Most readers, familiar with popular versions and parodies of this famous story, think that it is primarily a tale of split personality or schizophrenia. Actually, it is a valuable moral allegory about self-destructive compulsions that conquer and destroy a man's heartfelt desire to be good.

Discussion Starters: *How does this story merely exaggerate the truth that every man has both good and evil parts to himself? Why did Dr. Jekyll struggle so against Mr. Hyde? Can you think of thoughts or actions inside you that have shown both your "good" and "bad" sides?*

THE EDUCATION OF LITTLE TREE by Forrest Carter

An Indian boy learns what is required of a young man of integrity after suffering a family tragedy. Middle school curricula shouldn't overlook this book. It is a valuable, inspiring story about how a boy grows up in the face of adversity. Boys who are going through divorce, deaths in the family,

or other painful times will feel befriended by the book and also morally awakened.

Discussion Starters: *How does Little Tree learn much more than just the lessons of schooling? What are some of the lessons others might learn from Little Tree?*

THE GRAPES OF WRATH by John Steinbeck

A wonderful, heartbreaking story about the violence of poverty, John Steinbeck's unforgettable novel (see "100 Movies," page 50) has been, for generations, a crucial introduction to important social issues. Empathy, self-sacrifice, responsibility, and honor are all important character lessons in this story. *The Grapes of Wrath* contrasts man's inhumanity to man with the love and caring of a family trying to tough out very hard times. For many boys, this will be the first "big" book they've ever read.

Discussion Starters: *Has the Judd family done anything to deserve their fate? Other than just his initials, how is Jim Casey a Christ-like figure? Is it fair that some people should have enormous wealth while others starve?*

HARRY POTTER AND THE SORCERER'S STONE
by J. K. Rowling

In this magical tale, a boy becomes a wizard at twelve, an event that complicates his life but also gives it meaning. Harry Potter provides a role model of a boy who must grow into a life of purpose and courage. Boys will enjoy the further books in this series as well.

Discussion Starters: *Think about the word* wizard *and its other, less magical meanings. How does Harry use his powers to build up his moral/ethical self? If you had a wizard's power, what good things might you do?*

HATCHET by Gary Paulsen

An extremely popular adventure tale about a boy stranded alone in the Canadian wilderness with only a hatchet to help him survive, this book is one that boys frequently recommend to one another and that even nonreaders get pulled into. What is sometimes forgotten about this Newbery Honor Book is that the protagonist, Brian, has to deal not only with his situation but with thoughts about his parents' divorce and other problems in his life, too. Responsibility and self-reliance are at the core of this story.

Discussion Starters: *What do you think would be the most important "tool" to have if you were stranded in the wilderness? How does the boy grow up by the hardships he endured?*

THE HOBBIT (the series) by J.R.R. Tolkien

Through the magical journey of Bilbo Baggins, boys learn that power is dangerous and that even the best person can be corrupted by it. These four long books are for strong readers, but any boy capable of understanding the plot will be enchanted and thrilled and will never forget all the new friends, mentors, and teachers he meets within.

Discussion Starters: *Even though this is an "imaginary" land, what qualities of character do the hobbitts possess that you most admire? If you got a magic ring and could disappear whenever you wanted, when would you use it most? Does being brave mean that you can't ever be afraid?*

IF ROCK AND ROLL WERE A MACHINE by Terry Davis

This is an important, powerful story about the damage that can be inflicted on a young male spirit and his resilience in facing it. In Bert's long struggle for self-esteem and his final facing-down of the cruel teacher who hurt him, boys discover the chance of redemption and are inspired to a personal code of honor, self-respect, and honesty.

Discussion Starters: *Why was Mr. Pinkus so set on breaking Bert's spirit? Why do Bert's parents go along with Pinkus's plan? What is the most important thing that Bert "wins" in the end?*

JOHNNY TREMAIN by Esther Forbes

In this story about the American War of Independence, Johnny Tremain learns firsthand the principles for which our founding fathers risked their lives: values such as self-sacrifice, loyalty, and service, and the truth that a free humanity is worth fighting and dying for.

Discussion Starters: *Why do you think that the author shows some of the British soldiers as decent, honorable men? Does America still value freedom as much as it did during Johnny Tremain's life? If you could go back in history to any place and time, where would you go and why?*

JONATHAN LIVINGSTON SEAGULL by Richard Bach

As much as Jonathan Livingston Seagull wants to fit in with the rest of the flock, he even more desperately wants to be the greatest flier in all the world of gulls. He is every boy trying to find his limits, then surpass them. How much must one sacrifice to be the very best at anything? What are the costs of "going for it" all the way? These discussion starters will allow you and your ambitious son to prepare for the painful and often lonely journey that is a part of achieving excellence in any sphere of life (whether in sports, academics, or even socially).

KIM by Rudyard Kipling

This challenging book, most suitable for stronger readers, presents a clear picture of a young man's struggle between two competing values: patriotism and spirituality. Kim is the orphaned son of a British soldier in India, during the period when Great Britain still ruled it. Fluent in the native tongue of India, Kim is a perfect spy for the English, until he meets a Tibetan monk and realizes that there is much more to life

than spying. Kim has to examine a wide range of moral decisions and decide what kind of man he really wants to be.

Discussion Starters: *How is Kim's father a symbol for much that is wrong with colonial societies? Why does Kim feel that his spying is a good thing in the beginning? What did this story teach you about faith (that is, about belief in things that can't be "proven")?*

LORD OF THE FLIES by William Golding

In this classic novel of boys lost on an island without adult supervision, morality comes under assault in immensely powerful terms. This book is both an allegory of human fate and a very real possibility. As the boys stake out hierarchical territories, coddle and humiliate each other, and grossly forget what it means to be human, every reader is frightened by the naked possibilities of the human soul and challenged to search for higher order.

Discussion Starters: *Which of the boys are you most like? Must what happened on that island always be so when boys go unsupervised? If you said yes, explain why, and explore what urges you think are hidden within boys and men.*

THE MASTER PUPPETEER by Katherine Paterson, illustrated by Haru Wells

In this novel of eighteenth-century Japan, famine threatens thirteen-year-old Jiro's family with starvation, and Jiro must make important moral decisions about how far he can and should go to help them. Despite its ancient time and place, this story feels contemporary and frankly teaches boys strong lessons in self-sacrifice, loyalty, duty, and responsibility.

Discussion Starters: *Do you think Jiro should have turned in Saburo for the reward? Explain how Jiro and Kinshi's friendship helps them both to become better young men. What does this story teach you about balancing responsibilities in life?*

THE MOVES MAKE THE MAN by Bruce Brooks

Jerome Foxworthy is the only African-American student in a newly integrated junior high school. A bigoted coach denies him his fondest dream of playing basketball, but he barely has a chance to worry about this problem before he's forced to change every goal. His single-parent mother is injured, and Jerome and his siblings must assume the running of the household. Snatched from childhood, Jerome is forced to take on adult responsibilities—his priorities change, and the new priorities change him. This is an excellent story to teach boys responsibility, empathy, self-sacrifice, and loyalty.

Discussion Starters: *Can you think of times when circumstances have forced you to change your priorities? Have you ever had to sacrifice a part of your childhood to serve your family or someone else? If so, how did that make you feel?*

NOTHING BUT THE TRUTH by Avi

When Philip Malloy has a run-in with his high school English teacher (she has given him a D), he decides to annoy her. Humming instead of singing along during the national anthem is a clear violation of the rules, but when Philip is suspended for it, he claims he was singing patriotically. Media, school authorities, and others get involved, and soon things are out of control. This is an important book for boys who are asserting their need to individuate and learning the limits of resisting authority. It is about honesty, fairness, and the need to face the hypocrisy of both oneself and society at large.

Discussion Starters: *Was Philip's teacher out of line to punish him as she did? What lesson might Philip have learned if he had not decided to be so defensive?*

THE OLD MAN AND THE SEA by Ernest Hemingway

A man can be destroyed but never defeated. This is the primary lesson Hemingway wanted to teach in this simple story of a fisherman who catches a great marlin, only to lose it to sharks. This novella, perhaps better than any other work, teaches boys to assume that life is very hard sometimes—filled with disappointments and tragedy, through which a man does his best and takes pride in the strength of his efforts, regardless of the outcome.

Discussion Starters: *Can you think of a time where you were shocked that something good turned out badly? What does the character of the old man teach about courage and perseverance? Do you know a man like him?*

ORDINARY GENIUS: THE STORY OF ALBERT EINSTEIN
by Stephanie Sammartino McPherson

He was one of the greatest thinkers and scientists in all history, but Einstein also comes across in this sharp, intelligent, accessible biography not as larger than life but as very much a part of it. This great thinker's humility and curiosity, shown clearly here as dominant characteristics of his personality, were mixed in with his temperament of the questioner—always probing, always searching.

Discussion Starters: *How are honesty, decency, and service evident in Albert Einstein's personality? Do you agree that Einstein's greatest strength was his love of life and learning?*

THE PEARL by John Steinbeck

A simple and poor family finds a huge, rare, and beautiful pearl. How wonderful! they think, they'll be rich, and all of their problems will disappear. But money can't buy happiness, and just the opposite happens: The pearl brings nothing but heartache, disappointment, and grief. John Steinbeck's classic tale is timeless in its values and in its basic moral lesson: Great wealth should be judged not by the

amount of money we have, but by the safety and well-being of the people we love.

Discussion Starters: *How is the found pearl dangerous, a little bit like winning the lottery? Can you put a price tag on the well-being of the people you love?*

THE RED PONY by John Steinbeck

Although this story is filled perhaps more with heartbreak than joy (a sensitive boy might need a little more support as he's reading), few novels teach responsibility better than *The Red Pony.* The gift of a beautiful young colt turns out to be the catalyst for young Jody Tiflin's transition from the carefree life of a child into the hard realities of adulthood.

Discussion Starters: *In what ways is Jody thrilled to receive the gift of the red pony? Think about great gifts you've wanted, and how, upon receiving one, it has changed your life.*

ROBINSON CRUSOE by Daniel Defoe

One of the truly great adventure/survival stories of all time, it is hard to believe that Robinson Crusoe was written almost three hundred years ago. Its long popularity is no doubt attributable to the excitement of its plot, yet from beginning to end, this story is filled with important moral lessons. Ultimately, it depicts a man victorious over his own selfishness and pride.

Discussion Starters: *Would Robinson's life have been worse* *if he'd followed his father's advice and help? How well would you handle being all alone on a deserted island? What does Crusoe learn about the balance between self-reliance and social needs?*

RUNNING LOOSE by Chris Crutcher

In this powerful novel, Louie Banks learns, the hard way, how expensive it can be to stand up for your principles. A crazed win-at-all-costs coach drives him off his beloved football team, and Louie's girlfriend is tragically killed in a car crash. His journey through pain teaches boys valuable lessons about loyalty, honor, fairness, self-respect, and the difficult truth that life is *not* always fair.

Discussion Starters: *What quality in Louie Banks do you admire the most? Which adults do you think are the most admirable in this story? How does Louie's interest in long-distance running help him to overcome his feelings of rejection and loss?*

THE SHILOH TRILOGY by Phyllis Reynolds Naylor

Shiloh, Saving Shiloh, and *Shiloh Season* make up a trilogy of books involving early adolescent boys and a beagle named Shiloh, whom one boy rescues from an abusive owner. Their adventures teach boys a great deal about honor, integrity, and compassion.

Discussion Starters: *What do these great stories teach about loyalty and responsibility? Do you think that Shiloh's first owner should have lost the right to call Shiloh his dog? Does* Shiloh *help*

you to know what you would do if you ever saw an animal being mistreated?

SOUNDER by William H. Armstrong

This is a story about America's ignoble history of racism, yet it celebrates qualities that are more humanly universal than narrowly racist. Sounder is an old "coon dog" who is shot and maimed while trying to follow his master. In a quiet, faithful, and powerful narration, the eldest son of the family, who is searching for his father (the master) too, tells us of his and his family's struggle to survive. Respect, loyalty, self-sacrifice, responsibility, all set against a background of unconscionable meanness and cruelty, make *Sounder* an unforgettable story and one that boys may come back to again and again.

Discussion Starters: *How is the faithful dog Sounder a lot like the family in his love and dignity? As he searches for his father, the boy learns to read—why and how is this important to him?*

STAYING FAT FOR SARAH BYRNES by Chris Crutcher

Eric Calhoune is a typical high school "loser." He is fat and not very popular, and his best friend is the disfigured loner Sarah Byrnes. Eric figures out that the reason Sarah has let him into her world is that he's a loser. But when his talents as a swimmer make social acceptance possible, he's afraid of losing weight because, by becoming different from Sarah, his best friend, he'll lose her. With incredible intensity, this story evolves into a powerful lesson for young men about fairness, friendship, responsibility, and loyalty.

Discussion Starters: *Why do you think Sarah is such a tough person? Does Sarah's dad get what he deserves? What does this story teach you about the costs of friendship?*

STOTAN! By Chris Crutcher

A small team of high school swimmers in eastern Washington state accept the challenge of their coach to go through Stotan week, the most grueling five days of training, discipline, and hard work they've ever known. (A *stotan* is someone who shares in equal measure the quiet acceptance of a stoic and the passionate spirit of a Spartan.) The young men learn these qualities—the courage to fight through pain, the strength to put forth their greatest effort regardless of how emotionally difficult life might be, and the need for friends to love and be loved in return—through their personal sacrifices and their belief in themselves and each other.

Discussion Starters: *Why is something like Stotan Week the exact opposite of finding a shortcut? Were the guys in this story made stronger by what happened to Jeff? Even if you're not a swimmer or an athlete, can you think of an area of your life where you could become a stotan?*

WALT WHITMAN by Catherine Reef,
illustrated by Wendell Minor

Walt Whitman's relationships with his parents, siblings, friends, and most of all his times make this an important book for teaching boys lessons in fairness, empathy, and honor. Whitman's painful experiences as a healer in Civil War hospitals and his love of Lincoln and his country teach high and noble ideals.

Discussion Starters: *How did Whitman's service in the Civil War change him? What did Whitman think of Abraham Lincoln, and how did he feel after Lincoln was assassinated?*

A WIZARD OF EARTHSEA by Ursula K. Le Guin,
illustrated by Ruth Robbins

A boy who likes Harry Potter books will love the Earthsea Trilogy. The remarkable magical world invented by Le Guin allows the reader to identify deeply with the moral challenges that young Ged, the novel's protagonist, faces as he becomes a person of power.

Discussion Starters: *What if one day you realized that you had a gift of magical powers—what would you most want to do with them? Would you be able to control that gift until you learned to use it wisely? In everyday life, every boy has powers—what are yours, and how do you use them?*

High School

THE ADVENTURES OF HUCKLEBERRY FINN

by Mark Twain

Like nearly all of Mark Twain's books, this one is about people—most often boys and young men—trying to develop character in both ordinary and extraordinary circumstances. Huck Finn's story is worth mining not only for its humor but also for its finely interwoven moral dialogue about character and ethics.

Discussion Starters: *How is Huck a victim of his times? How is he not? How does his journey down the river change his attitudes toward the slave Jim?*

AN AMERICAN MYSTIC by Michael Gurian

Ben Brickman, a spiritually minded young psychology student, is asked by a former mentor to investigate a bizarre spiritual phenomenon on the Aegean coast of Turkey. Ben's adventure is tutored by Joseph Kader, a Turkish mystic who holds many of the keys to the strange puzzle, among them the idea that every man, to fully become himself, must make the journey to enlightenment in his own way. This novel challenges older high school readers to ask some of the large spiritual questions.

Discussion Starters: *What does it mean to be a person of faith? How is humility essential for true success in life? How is being a man not just a psychological or social phenomenon but also a spiritual one?*

BILLY BUDD by Herman Melville

Billy Budd is a young sailor who accidentally kills a cruel, false accuser. Although the captain of the ship understands Billy's act, he still must decide whether to execute him. Tense and filled with questions of morality and values, *Billy Budd,* like a few other great books from the time period when it was written (*The Scarlet Letter* comes instantly to mind), wrestles with the grand questions of life. These grand questions are great discussion starters.

Discussion Starters: *What is right and wrong? How do we right wrongs? What does a good man do when faced with evil?*

BLACK LIKE ME by John Howard Griffin

A white man in 1950s America dyes his skin dark to find out what life is like for a "Negro" in the American South. The horrors of racism that he encounters, both the blatant examples and the subtle ones, make for a horrible, soul-wrenching experience. Reading this powerful novel, which is based on a true story, young men learn the unfairness, meanness, and ignorance of racial prejudice and the cost to individuals and society alike when such racism exists.

Discussion Starters: *How can you combat racism in your life? How does Griffin's story show what empathy is?*

BRAVE NEW WORLD by Aldous Huxley

In a world engineered for comfort, convenience, and being "happy," what could go wrong? A great deal, once one man starts making waves. This essential novel inspires young men to realize that choosing their conscience and thinking for themselves can be costly, but that human life depends on our paying that cost. Written as a satire of a society ever more eager to eliminate hardship by eliminating freedom, the brave new world of Huxley's vision forces boys to think about their independence, their integrity, and whether "fitting in" is as important as they might think.

Discussion Starters: *What is basically wrong with the brave new world described in this story? Can you have freedom without there being a chance of difficulties?*

THE CATCHER IN THE RYE by J. D. Salinger

Holden Caulfield, a voice not just of his 1950s generation but arguably of *all* generations of teenage boys, discovers that life is increasingly complicated and difficult after quitting school. Holden is the personification of empathy, and his sense of honesty, decency, and fairness shine through even the most self-absorbed moments of his story.

Discussion Starters: *Why does Holden run away from school? Which parts of his personality do you like most, his kindness or his sharp sarcastic wit? Explain what Holden says about a "catcher in the rye." How does this explanation show the depth of Holden's kindness and sense of fairness?*

CHINESE HANDCUFFS by Chris Crutcher

Terrible things happen in life sometimes, especially to young people, and the cliché "That which doesn't kill you, makes you stronger" is not only true but also reminds us how unfair life can feel. In *Chinese Handcuffs,* this lesson is powerfully revealed in the struggle of the protagonist, Dillon Hemingway, to rescue his friend, Jennifer Lawless, from a terrifying situation of sexual abuse.

Discussion Starters: *What would you do if someone you loved told you a terrible secret about their life and asked you not to tell? Why is it especially unfair for an adult to be sexual with a child? Is a novel like this one a good place to learn empathy for people who have suffered terrible pain?*

THE CHOSEN by Chaim Potok

Once a high-school-age boy, or a mature middle school reader, discovers Potok's books, he may not rest until he reads them all. *The Chosen* is still considered Potok's classic, and for good reason. This story of Jewish boys growing up in New York has become a universal tale of all boys who seek their own individuality both with and without the blessings of their families and religious traditions. Friends Reuven and Danny struggle together to discover a spiritual and moral center.

Discussion Starters: *What does this story teach about the conflict between being a good, dutiful son and being your own person? How do the two main characters become friends? Why might one call this a book mostly about honor?*

DAVID COPPERFIELD by Charles Dickens

"I am born," begins this tale of cruelty and hardship and, ultimately, of the people and spirit that save a child. Dickens said that the moral of this story was the old axiom "Do unto others as you would have them do unto you"—a lesson he learned during his own childhood years of abuse and neglect, and a lesson that David Copperfield learns in this wonderful, heartfelt story.

Discussion Starters: *Why were people so mean to David Copperfield? Imagine what it would be like to live in an orphanage where the people in charge didn't care about you. Do you see*

how child welfare laws help protect children and why such laws are needed? Explain.

THE DIARY OF A YOUNG GIRL by Anne Frank

Anne Frank lived her short life with enormous personal integrity. Her death, only a few months before the Allied liberation of Holland, where she and her family had been hiding from the Nazis for over two years, was deeply tragic. But the journal she left behind, filled with typical teenage concerns and a horrifyingly beautiful understanding of the moral challenges of life, has inspired millions of readers and become the conscience of a generation.

Discussion Starters: *How did Anne Frank feel about her life situation? Can you imagine a society where you had to live in such terrible conditions, just because of your ethnicity?*

ENDER'S GAME by Orson Scott Card

This classic science fiction novel, like Card's *Seventh Son,* an equally powerful fantasy novel, begins a series of novels in which boys grow to manhood by discovering and accepting their moral and spiritual destinies. Every moral competency is covered in these books, in the same way that C. S. Lewis was able to create a drama that seemed to absorb every key theme of human development. A Mormon, Card imbues his vision with virtue and values, yet like Lewis, he never becomes overwhelmed by doctrine or proselytizing.

While each book in Card's series is a good template for moral discussion, classrooms will probably benefit most from the first in each series. Some students will get "hooked" and pursue the others themselves.

Discussion Starters: *What do these books teach about honor? Empathy? Responsibility? How do these stories show that some parts of morality are absolute and cross all cultures and philosophies, while others are relative and situational?*

EXODUS by Leon Uris

In this thrilling epic story about the settling of the modern Jewish country of Israel, Uris captures grand human events as seen through the eyes of ordinary people who rise to honor and heroism. *Mila 18, Trinity, Battle Cry,* and many other Uris books are wonderful for teaching young people about ethics and personal integrity. Uris's *The Haj* is a very powerful book written from the Palestinian point of view.

Discussion Starters: *Why was the state of Israel a necessity not only for the Jews but for modern civilization? Would you act like Dov if you were in his place? Do you feel loyalty to any person, place, or group like the modern-day Israelis feel?*

GREAT EXPECTATIONS by Charles Dickens

In this classic Dickens novel, the uprooted young Pip struggles to separate right from wrong and to reclaim himself. This is one of Dickens's greatest books, sometimes senti-

mental but always unfolding around a core of value-oriented themes, including decency, self-sacrifice, honesty, and honor.

Discussion Starters: *What is Pip's initial attraction to the wealthy Miss Havisham based on? Why do you think Magwitch was willing to help Pip without thanks or appreciation? Explain what you think is Pip's most important life lesson.*

THE JUNGLE by Upton Sinclair

The Jungle is a painful and at times horrible story of the struggle of immigrants to America during the early twentieth century. It shows our sons the ugliness and danger of the stockyards of Chicago before there was such a thing as the Food and Drug Administration, and the ways in which the America of that era allowed for the horrendous exploitation of people who only wanted to work hard and earn a decent living. Issues of fairness, self-sacrifice, service, and responsibility are powerfully presented throughout this tough, important story.

Discussion Starters: *As time passes, how does Jurgis change in his attitudes toward standing on his own? Explain why this novel is such a powerful example of unfairness.*

NIGHT by Elie Wiesel

Wiesel has written a work of extraordinary beauty, power, and pain about his time in a concentration camp at age ten.

His story, despite its horrors and terror, is one of mystical beauty, portraying the human spirit surviving its encounter with true evil. Respect, empathy, decency, honesty, and honor are the all-important moral elements of this superb memoir.

Discussion Starters: *Why is it so important that we never forget the lessons of the Holocaust? Discuss evil and meanness in society—how did Germany in the 1930s and 1940s allow itself to become so evil? How do you think Wiesel would define the word* character?

OF MICE AND MEN by John Steinbeck

Lenny is a developmentally handicapped "giant" whose sweet disposition ill prepares him to live in the world of greed, selfishness, and cruelty. George, no match for Lenny physically, is of normal intelligence and tries to watch out for and take care of his friend. Heartbreaking and filled with scene after scene of poignant, ironic moments, *Of Mice and Men* is considered by some to be a nearly perfect novel of friendship and moral development.

Discussion Starters: *How are Lenny's constant references to "living off the fat of the land" intended as ironic? Why might Lenny, who is such a simple person, be considered a "better" man than some of the other characters in this story? In the end, can you see why the terrible action that George must take is an act of love?*

ONE DAY IN THE LIFE OF IVAN DENISOVICH
by Alexander Solzhenitsyn

In this straightforward, powerful message of spiritual strength and personal dignity, Ivan Denisovich is just an average man who is a political prisoner in one of Stalin's Siberian gulags. He comes to understand that even when everything else is stripped from a man, that man still has himself.

Discussion Starters: *If you were unfairly imprisoned, how long would it take you to make the best of your situation? How did Ivan Denisovich maintain his dignity? Would you rather be imprisoned wrongly but know that you are innocent, or "get away" with a terrible crime and live your whole life in the knowledge of your guilt?*

THE PAINTED BIRD by Jerzy Kosinski

A young gypsy boy uses every bit of wit and ingenuity he can muster to survive the terrors of World War II in Eastern Europe. Shifted from uncaring family to uncaring family, always close to starvation or imprisonment and execution by the Nazis, the ten-year-old boy grows up very quickly. This violent and painful story nonetheless presents important lessons in decency, kindness (and the lack thereof), and empathy. *The Painted Bird,* Kosinski's greatest work, grew out of true-life experiences. Be sure to discuss with your sons the Afterword and Kosinski's thoughts about his life.

Discussion Starters: *How does the boy first realize how desperate his situation is? The things this boy sees—can you imagine being his age and seeing such things? How would that change your views of the world?*

THE RED BADGE OF COURAGE by Stephen Crane

Stephen Crane's Civil War story of the young soldier Henry Fleming is much more than just another tale about the horrors of war. Yet *The Red Badge of Courage* hardly qualifies as a story about heroes and bravery either, as Henry has his share of cowardly moments and makes poor decisions. In the end, it is a truthful account of how our hopes and dreams change with the passage of time and the gaining of moral experiences.

Discussion Starters: *Can you forgive Henry his moments of "cowardice"? What is a "red badge of courage," and how does Henry's view of it change as he further experiences war? Can you imagine a situation where it would take even more courage* not *to fight in a war than it would to fight?*

THE SCARLET LETTER by Nathaniel Hawthorne

The characters of Chillingworth and Dimmesdale, in opposing ways, fail to find their moral center when their society does not help them do so. Hester Prynne, on the other hand, not only finds her own moral center but holds fast to it.

Discussion Starters: *What does this novel show about the*

lack of Christian kindness and forgiveness in Puritan society? How does Hester prove that her sense of right and wrong comes from within, not from what others say about her? Think of a time when you've had to take a stand against something you knew was wrong, even though others disagreed with you.

A SEPARATE PEACE by John Knowles

This powerful novel tells the story of two young men, best friends, in the days just before World War II. With the horror of war inevitably hovering, Gene and Finny live hard, play hard, and make choices with all the carelessness of youth. But certain of their choices lead to immense pain, and they must face the consequences. An excellent opportunity to teach boys the costs of friendship and how truly hard and painful some of life's lessons can be, this book, although sad and disturbing, is a crucial moral allegory.

Discussion Starters: *What are the worst mistakes that Gene and Finny make in their friendship? How does the coming of war change Gene and help him see inside himself?*

SIDDARTHA by Hermann Hesse

This story of a young man's spiritual and moral development is loosely based on the life of the Buddha. Few novels match it for moral and spiritual content. A young man who is clearly touched by this book ought also to be provided with Hesse's *Narcissus and Goldmund*. Because of the sophistication of language, Hesse's books are best read by very mature high school readers.

Discussion Starters: *Why do you think Siddartha finds peace and enlightenment before his friend who becomes a monk, even though Siddartha does not follow a narrow path of study? What do you think "enlightenment" would feel like? In what way can we say that everyone, including you, is a prophet?*

SOPHIE'S WORLD by Jostein Gaarder

Sophie's life changes one day when she receives two questions in the mail: Who are you? and where does the world come from? Her suspenseful search for the answers to these questions inspires young adults (and adults) to ask the questions for themselves and make their own search. This book is just right for high-school-age boys who lean a little toward the philosophical.

Discussion Starters: *What similar "big ideas" have you considered yourself? Explain how considering such fundamental questions helps a boy to grow up and take his place in the adult world.*

STRANGER IN A STRANGE LAND by Robert A. Heinlein

Along with other classics like Isaac Asimov's *Foundation*, Ursula K. Le Guin's *The Left Hand of Darkness*, and Philip K. Dick's *The Man in the High Castle*, this science fiction novel creates a world in which boys and men face immense life-challenges. The young man who likes one of these

books will like them all. The best science fiction literature is some of the most morally challenging that humanity has ever produced. In Heinlein's book, human civilization both deifies and then destroys a Christ-like "Martian." A journalist and many other individuals participate in both the glamour and the gluttony that a "great person" inspires, and all discover in the end how flawed we are, and how vigilant we must be in our individual and collective searches to do the right thing.

Discussion Starters: *The title comes from the Bible—who was the "stranger in a strange land" in the Bible? Is the sacrifice at the end inevitable, given what you know about humanity? Or can you see another realistic ending?*

THINGS FALL APART by Chinua Achebe

When one culture colonizes another, one of life's greatest moral questions emerges: Is freedom due only to the mighty? This touching novel follows the life of Okonkwo, a respected leader of his tribe who must struggle with the colonizing Christian missionaries in Nigeria in the early 1800s. A powerful tale of one man's sense of service, empathy, self-sacrifice, and self-respect, this story highlights the well-intentioned Euro-Christian culture's clash with tribal traditions and illustrates how a colonial power, like a bully, can destroy others instead of facing its own confusions and pride head on.

Discussion Starters: *Were the Euro-Christians responsible* *for Okonkwo's death? Do good intentions negate bad results? How does this story change your perspective on history? In what ways will this book change your tolerance of other customs and cultures?*

TO KILL A MOCKINGBIRD by Harper Lee

In one of the most important novels of the twentieth century (see also movie on page 41), a father is at the center of racial strife in a southern town. His children, too, wrestle with some of the most important issues of growing up. Courage, conviction, moral duty, compassion—all are tested. Racism becomes a topic in discussions about this book, in a way that guides young people deep into their own prejudices and intrinsic desires to do what's right.

Discussion Starters: *How does the character of Boo Radley work as an example of some moral values (like honor, decency, and kindness)? Racial strife continues to exist in our society, but how have things improved?*

TUESDAYS WITH MORRIE by Mitch Albom

The subtitle to this very readable true story is *An old man, a young man, and life's greatest lesson.* Seventy-plus-year-old Morrie, who is dying of Lou Gehrig's disease, teaches Albom, his former student, many important lessons. Respect, honor, empathy, indeed virtually every moral competency is revealed as Morrie courageously faces his death, all the while mentoring the spirit of the living.

Discussion Starters: *How does Mitch believe he and Morrie drifted apart? Explain Morrie's attitudes toward service and helping others. Why might you say that Morrie's greatest gift to Mitch is the gift of love?*

WATERSHIP DOWN by Richard Adams

Fiver, the mystic of a group of rabbits living in the English countryside, foresees disaster coming. He implores the leader of the rabbits, Hazel, to guide them to a new place to live. This powerful story is, at its heart, about justice, peace, and the preciousness of our environment. Ultimately, it is about self-sacrifice for the good of the community. The fact that it is stirring, exciting, and tense is just icing on the cake.

Discussion Starters: *How does this story suggest that sometimes "development" is not the best thing? Are there parts of your environment that you hope will never be bulldozed away? What does this story teach about politics?*

Alphabetical Index of All Movies

Alphabetical Index of All Books

About the Authors

Michael Gurian is a family therapist, educator, and author of twelve books, including the bestsellers *The Wonder of Boys, a Fine Young Man,* and *The Good Son.* He is credited with first bringing the boys movement to public attention. His work has been featured in nearly all the national media, including The *New York Times, USA Today,* the *Today Show,* and PBS. He lives in Spokane, Washington, with his wife, Gail, who is also a family therapist, and their two children.

Terry Trueman has been a teacher for almost thirty years and is the author of the young readers novel *Stuck in Neutral,* as well as *Sheehan.* For five years he produced reviews and criticism of films, videos, and books on the NPR affiliate KPBX. Terry, the father of two sons, lives in Spokane, Washington.

With any comments, please write to Michael Gurian at:
P.O. Box 8714
Spokane, WA 99203
www.michael-gurian.com
Write to Terry at:
tet@uswest.net

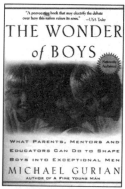

The Wonder of Boys

"The impetus behind a growing 'boys movement.'" —*USA Today*

"Full of good insights and advice." —*Los Angeles Times*

A Fine Young Man

"Convincingly illustrates the peculiar pain the potential loneliness of being a boy in America today." —*Time*

"Filled with stories and practical advice for parents and teachers of adolescent boys." —Mary Pipher, author *Reviving Ophelia*

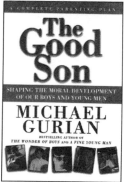

The Good Son
A Complete Parenting Plan

"A crucial addition to our arsenal of resources to improve the odds for youth." —Thomas M. McKenna, National Executive Director, Big Brothers Big Sisters of America